BOLESLAW   TABOR

The truth

like

a poke in the eye

The truth like a poke in the eye

by

Boleslaw Tabor

First Edition

Published by:

Lulu Inc.

www.lulu.com

Cover designed by:

Boleslaw Tabor

ISBN: 978-1-105-38555-1

Table of Contents

Introduction

From the author

Just a few words about myself.

I'm working on my first book. It is very hard and I progress very slowly. I'm kind of proud of myself for doing it. When I finish I'm going to read the second one and later who knows maybe one more.

Dedication

I dedicate this book to everybody who was inspiration for me and to those whose characters and behaviors are described in the book.

Preface

When I've stopped working it turned out I have much more time to think about many situations around us.

I have never been interested in politics at all. After the September 2001 it was hard to not think about it. I've been listening to the media talking about various subjects mostly about economics and I had a feeling it is all about something else than the media are telling us. It happened to me to have discussions with my friends on similar subjects and I usually had different opinion than they had. When we think about something usually we reach too soon shallow conclusions. In such case there is no chance to dig dipper into the subject. Later on I began to reconsider the same mostly economical problems writing down on the paper all numbers. I wanted to understand the proportions, reasons, causes. Writing down is forcing us to a level of systematic research and gives us additional time to reconsider all numbers and what they mean.

At that time I've noticed the numbers are giving additional light to the problems and many subjects look completely different in the new light. I began own research by reading articles, watching programs, searching on the internet too. It is obvious to everybody that media are not for informing people. The main purpose of the media is to push required by the media owner opinion into us consciously or unconsciously. When media are repeating the same opinion about any subject too often we can be sure it is not even close to the truth. In last couple of years media are telling us how stimulus programs are causing inflation. It seams to be reasonable but since media are saying it we know for sure it is not truth and in reality it is about something else.

I began to count and recounct banks debts, debts of people paying mortgages and it turned out that banks never lose in any situation. Anyway a couple of years earlier I noticed banks have changed rules for approving mortgages. It ment that behind our backs the masters of the world are planning something. I didn't know what the planning could be about and I didn't have any time or curiosity to investigate it farther. Later when I began thinking about it I considered what means for any currency to have coverage of gold. After long recounting and considerations and attempts to discus this subject with friends in my view showed up a new picture of economy.

One aspect in just one single situation on let's say American market is tightly related to many other aspects and I had to at least briefly research many subjects. After reaching the first conclusions I was writing down my observations and later when reached different conclusions I could modify my previous ones. All writings were chaotic and split into tiny pieces what made more difficult to check and compare my current opinions with the previous ones. At such point I had to put it all into one bigger document.

In the next period of time when from time to time I've got any new observations or conclusions I was adding it to the main document. This document was keep growing. All of it is not very systematic nor has pin point accuracy and many considerations are assuming average realistic values appropriate to the subject of consideration. The numbers and the conditions I was using have large enough margin of error to make sure I was not twisting facts. I believe solely that if anyone corrects my numbers to the real accurate values from real cases the conclusions are going to stay the same.

My opinions and conclusions are very controversial and most often opposite to the commonly accepted ones. It is like that mostly because most people have no time to think and make own consideration and they just repeat what they hear and see and what seams to be about right. Passing by from mouth to mouth every story is getting more and more colorful and grows with details. When the story goes around and comes to the original story teller it fits original concept and even the person who made it up starts assuming it is the truth and whole truth.

There are plenty of false common opinions believed to be truth but most of us would never admit it is false and we are keep telling to ourselve that what we say is the truth. It happens in the media and on the internet and Youtube that someone is touching the same subject giving us additional light. Unfortunately it cannot be the whole truth because if it would be the truth than it would be removed from the media immediately and the author would be in very big trouble. It is the same on every public level. Those who fight with "the evil" or anything what is wrong are doing it only a little bit and they never tell publicly about obvious easy to check facts because they would be punished for it severly.

For the people who have never considered much all touched by me subjects at first glance might feel like a poke in the eye. And, I 've just got the title for my book.

I wish everybody is serious thinking about what is going on around us. I hope the increase of knowledge could one day save us from very dire straits.

American dollar and almost all about it.

Introduction to thoughts about currencies.

Just about one month before the year 2002 when I was already not working there was a program on TV channel PBS about those who print American money. Thanks that all came together in my mind.

I've seen a movie about money on Youtube.
The author is very nicely and precisely telling between minute 23 and minute 25 what I was chaotically repeating for some time.
It is like in example with bank, builder, construction worker, house where money were created from nothing but everything is working like in machine because bank employees do not understand anything and they are just making sure that left side is equal the right side.
The same way as I write about a big businessman who when in need for money tells the president to give him. Since president does not have money then the businessman is printing the new money and lending it to the president.
It is like in the old Polish joke when Kobuszewski is asking a question "Since the Poland has debts, Germany has debts, Rusia has debts, Anerica has debts than with whom they are all in debts?". There you have the answer. Someone made up and printed money from paper in other words made something from nothing and lent it to others.

In the farther part of the Youtube movie I disagree with the author. Firstly the world grew much bigger then we have much more transactions and we need much more money to use in all transactions. When there is introduced us much new money as bigger is economical world the inflation is not growing. Secondly coverage in gold means little because at one time a piece of gold is worth a suit and shoes but at another time like during the WWII the same piece was worth a piece of bread for a child. On the other hand the gold as money is no different than a piece of paper as money since gold as it is has very little real value (maybe except couple of electronic connectors).

Someone has to introduce the currency to the market. It must by someone very powerful who is able to stabilize the value of the currency (to prevent someone else from introducing other money or someone who can prove that other money is less valuable). They wanted to have rights to print money to become very powerful (positive feedback theory?). It is not truth that those who can print money are rich because can print as much as they want. They are rich because they are powerful and they are powerful because they decide how much new money to print and how much old money to shread.

Another thing is if the dollar would be changed to constitutional then at once there is a problem on the world market. Let's say someone from France would sell something in the USA and received American currency. For American currency the person could buy only things in the USA. There is the same in case of any two countries. Right now when American Dollar is an international currency someone from Germany can sell goods to Spain and receive American Dollar and then use it to buy goods in Finland.

There is no difference if the currency is constitutional, government issued, gold or whatever. The only difference would be exchanging goods or services for goods or for services. Can you imagine buying personally roses in Africa?

On the other hand in case currency like dollar would be owned by government than everyone in government would print for himself or herself as much as possible to make sure they can grab it all because after the election those people are replaced by another money printing and grabbing people. Right now American Dollar is in privete hands and those people are taking care of it. It is something like dynasty and everybody cares to keep power and pass it from father to son and they are forced to keep dollar strong.

We could see a trend when riches are going to live in palaces and poor are going to work hard. It was always like that. The riches are stronger more powerful and they can do whatever they want. This is the main purpose of creating countries for powerful, rich, privileged people to give them wealth, privileges ... enforced by the police and the army. Nothing new under the sun.

The man in the Youtube video didn't menmtion that the only purpose of stock exchanges is to create corrections or huge fall downs. Any small or big correction is taking from the poorer and giving to the richer. The corrections are moving money and shares from poorer to the richest and then the money can be taken off from the circulation, let's call it shreading.

Changing current leaders for other leaders? What could it do? Maybe a bit because the new broom is sweeping better at the beginning. People are like most animals. They like to live in groups and they need any leaders who would tell them what to do. The leader will always benefit more and more until the people start uprising, change leader for new ones and the story starts from beginning.

There is a lot of truth in the Youtube movie but not the whole truth.

A lot of noise about money.

Lately I began to be intrigued by the money.

Let's consider the green buck without taking in count what influence it has on people.

Generally there is a lot of talk these days about how the stimulus is creating inflation and that green buck is losing its value. Somehow you can't really see it. There is always the case that when the media are saying something it is all about something else. I began thinking without much knowledge about the subject. We all usually are in a situation and we are considering what to do from that point of view because we want to get the best results in any case. Very often our current position is so unclear with relation to the true perspectives that we don't really know what to think.

The property tax is an excellent example. When people have no money to pay the property tax then someone is making a strange move to give people hope and get them to the voting polls. Year or two later this good looking move will kick those people even more severly. The truth is property tax is paying for things not related to properties at all then home value should never ever be taken in consideration. This is another story all together.

Let's go back to the green thing.

At the introduction everybody should know that printed buck is not important. Important is to prove that you are or were in possession of it. I heard that right before WWII and right after the war some people were going to the American Ambassy with suitcases of dollars. They were burning it there and receiving certificate stating amount burned. Later they were leaving to US and there they were receiving equal amount of dollars although it was forbidden to carry US dollars through the border.

Did people lose houses because of subprime mortgages?

The whole story is only to make a noise. All those mortgages were with very little or no down payment. People taking those loans at that time could not afford to buy a house and only thanks to the subprime mortgages they made purchases and lived in those houses for few years. They can keep living in there if they can keep making payments. If they cannot keep paying monthly payments they have to move out but as I said before they lived there for few years only because of those subprimes. In reality those people didn't lose anything but they gained the most.

The only once who could lose on those loans are people who already lived in the houses with large equities but not understanding what is going on they changed regular ruled mortgages for subprime mortgages. Then after few years of paying off they've got bigger debt than before payments. When at the same time the house value dropped down below a critical point those people might not be able to renew their mortgages. I don't think there is many such cases and if they are they should blame own greed and ignorance.

Is banking system going to bankruptcy because of people's problems with paying mortgages?

So we are told the banks are going down on a big scale because of mortgages. Let's consider one example.

We start with simple beginning.

A builder want's to build a house. He borrows $300,000 from a bank. The interest is 5%.

$300,000 left from the bank.

The builder pays all those money to construction worker and in 3,4 years the house is finished.

The house is for sale for $600,000. This house can be bought by the construction worker because in our world he is the only one with money earned by building the house. To buy the house the worker needs to borrow additional $300,000 with interest 5% from the bank.

At this point $600,000 left from the bank.

The worker payes the builder money borrowed from the bank plus all earning. The builder pays off own loan plus interest giving the bank back $345,000.

After the transaction there is $255,000 out from bank. The money has the builder and the worker owns the house.

The times are bad. The builder hardly ever hires worker and during 4 years the worker is able to earn only $83,700. The worker is paying of the interest only and finaly he goes bankrupt and the bank is doing foreclosure.

The worker paid back $83,700 and still has $216,300 debt.

At this point $171,300 left the bank. The money is in hands of the builder.

The bank is taking over the house and selling it. In our world only the builder has money and is buying the house for $171,300.

Please note that the worker debt was $216,300 but bank recovered only $171,300.

After the transaction all money came back to the bank. The builder owns the house. The worker is out on the street.

Assuming the cost to build the house was $300,000 and the house was at one point worth $600,00 on the market and price dropped down it was sold for $171,300 it is all possible although the numbers are extreme.

All money coming out of the bank:

+$300,000(loan for the builder + $300,000(loan for the worker to purchase the house) - $345,000 (the builder paying back the loan + interest) - $83,700(interest paid by worker) - $171,300(the house bank sale) = 0

All money received by the builder:

$300,000(loan from the bank) - $300,000(worker's salary during building the house) + $600,000(the house sale) - $345,000(paying back loan + interest) - $83,700(worker's salary in the later years) - $171,300(purchasing the house) = 0

All money received by the worker:

+$300,000(salary during building of the house) + $300,000(loan from the bank) - $600,000(purchasing the house) + $83,700(salary in the later years) - $83,700(paying back the interest) = 0

I know the worker has to eat and purchase other things too. We could assume the worker earned money for food and other things somewhere else. We can say builder paid for the land and materials using the money earned somewhere else or decrease the final house price.

In this case I wanted to demonstrate how our very small financial world is operating for about 8 years only. The bank printed money from nothing and later took all of its money back and destroyed it. The bank situation has not changed because it has nothing at the end like nothing at the beginning. Although the worker is out on the street one house was built.

I know the prices of the houses were keep growing but usually is that people borrow at least 75% for the small house. Later they sell it and they borrow at least 75% of the value of their bigger house. In such case the sum of loans (amount of money coming out of the banks) is growing but people are paying more debts off (money is coming back to the banks). In result amount of debts is growing and amount of paid off debts is growing. When house values are growing slower than interests more money is coming back to the banks than leaving banks. Let's say a house has the price $500,000 and interest is 5%. Let's see if the house price went up $25,000 in the first year, $26,250 the second year, $27,560 the third year. In three years the house values has to go up to $578,812. Years ago the interest was much higher than we can easily assume the house prices could double in 10 years and quadruple in 20 years. Anyway with such speed of grow all money is coming back to the banks. When I was buying the first house I calculated that when you borrow $200,000 you have to pay back about $450,000. The conclusion is more money is coming back to the banks than going out of the banks.

The media informed us lately that 69% of US population live in their houses but only 10% of them has paid of mortgage. It means 69-7=62% has a mortgage. The great depression and wars were long time ago and that people's standard went up in the nineties. The longer people are working the more loan they have paid off. The people borrow more and more to buy bigger and bigger house but only to the point when they get the most expensive house they could have in their lives. Later they don't change houses because they don't need to. The babyboomers (born after the WWII) already began changing their houses for smaller, less expensive. Since we have to Pay back 2-2.5 times more than we borrow the mortgages are causing the most money is coming back to the banks after 10 years. Am I right?

The world market is growing and we need more money on the market.

We need more and more money until we have more than we can spend.

From this point it is more important to keep control and make sure that we as well as our children will always have more than it is possible to spend. For such people the money is not important anymore. They can destroy all excessive money if they want. It is similar to the coffee from Brasil. It was better to load the ship with coffee and dump it in Atlantic Ocean and keep the high price than carry it to the destination country and sell it for much lower price.

From mortgage consideration we see that problems like those right now are the best way to take money from the market and leave people on the street like the construction worker.

The main purpose of stock exchanges is to keep inflation in check.

A stock exchange is the next case for consideration.

People are trading on stock exchanges. Someone is lucky and gains but the most gains have those who can manipulate with prices. I think those who print US Dollar can speculate easily because as I said earlier they do not need money. They suck it from the traders and then they remove it form the world market by destroying the excess.

 The share is an imaginary unit describing proportional ownership of the company. As the imaginary unit it has no dollar value at all. We need to realize that share price has nothing to do with company issuing that share. It has nothing to do neither with condition nor financials of the firm. The shares are important for the company only at the beginning when they are issued. When a firm needs money it issues pieces of paper called shares to give some ownership to those who bring money to the firm. The firm doesn't care if they issue 100 share $1 each or 20 shares $5 each. In both cases the firm would receive $100 of the investors' money with exchange for tiny portion of the ownership.

We should never thing that those who purchase shares are really investors. The true investors are only those who own controlling number of shares. Those who control the firm, never ever bnenefit from the shares directly. They just decide to give themselves, they associates higly paid positions, bonuses and benefits. All other shareholders are just speculators with hope that those worthless pieces of paper called shares could be sold for the higher price than they purchased them.

Let's see an example.

Once upon a time a firm issued one share for $100. Mr. X purchased it and the money was used by the firm in good or bad manner.

Let's say in our world exists one share only and there is only $110.

Later in time on the market there is one share and its price is $100.

Mr. X has one share and $0, Mr. Y has $100 and Mr. Z has $10.

In total they have $110 and one share.

Mr. X is selling the share to Mr. Y for $100.

After the transaction Mr. X has $100, Mr. Y has 1 share and Mr. Z has $10.

In total they have $110 and 1 share.

After some time the share value drops down to $10 because very rich Mr. X does neither want nor needs to buy the share and Mr. Z cannot afford to pay more than that. Mr. Y sells the share to Mr. Z. Mr. Y lost $90.

After the transaction Mr. X has $100, Mr. Y has $10 and Mr. Z has 1 share.

In total they have $110 and 1 share.

Mr. Y just sold his share then he cannot buy it back. At this time Mr. X offers $1 for the share and he waits. Sooner or later Mr. Z would have to sell the share. And he does.

After the transaction Mr. X has $99 and 1 share, Mr. Y has $10 and Mr. Z has $1.

In total they have $110 and 1 share.

Mr. X says and media repeats after him the share is worth $90 now. Nobody is buying but people think it could be the truth. It looks like prices are jumping up and down a lot. People hope the price would drop down and they could buy it.

Later on Mr. X decides the share price is $30, later $20 and finaly $9. At this point Only Mr. Y has such money and he thinks it is very good price. He hopes to wait until price go up and sell it with profit. He makes decision and buys the share.

After the transaction Mr. X has $108, Mr. Y has $1 and 1 share, Mr. Z has $1.

In total there is $110 and 1 share on the market.

There is recession and hard times for people now. Nobody except very rich Mr. X can afford to pay for the share more than $1. Mr. X takes his time and waits. When he thinks the time is right he offers $2 for the share to make sure nobody else could get the share. He makes the purchase.

After the transaction Mr. X has $106 and 1 share, Mr. Y has $2 and Mr. Z has $1.

In total there is $110 and 1 share.

Now we have special situation on the market. The share as well as most of the money is in one hand of very rich Mr. X. This situation is colled correction on stock exchange. Most people lost money and they don't have neither money nor shares. The very rich Mr. X does not need money and he can take most of his $106 out of the circulation and shred it. His action reducing amount of the money on the market prevents the inflation.

We know now it doesn't matter if share prices are going up or down there is always constant amount of money on the market. Someone loses are someone elses gains. Share price manipulation has nothing to do with issuing company at all. Because of that it should be forbidden to trade shares and to speculate on stock exchange.

The fact the firm can issue the shares and buy back the shares is not important and has no relation to the share price. Sure it has to be marketed right. The share price would matter for the firm only when the firm would be buying back all its shares but it never happens.

Coming back to our misters we have Mr. X who has more money than he needs and he can destroy excess of the money (money he printed before). All transactions and speculations reduced amount of the money on the market.

One additional aspect to the firm is it sometimes earns money and cannot do much with it. It is not right to pay to the director owner because of lots of taxes have to be paid. It is no good idea to keep as retaining earning because lots of taxes would have to be paid. There is nothing to invest at this point and no way to expand. Dividends cannot be paid because who is so stupid to pay strange people so called investors with proportion to the number of owned shares. In such case the firm is buying back the shares to discard them. In this case the lower the share's price the better because for the same amount of money the firm can get rid of larger number of shares. Removing larger number of shares leaves more percentage of shares to the controlling sherholder real owner.

The conclusion is the stock market correction has the only purpose to take money from general population and discard it to keep inflation in check

Export import.

Media say USA is importing much more than they are exporting then American Dollar is going out of the country on the world market and it is lowering its value. Yeaa, you could think so, but....

Some time ago the powerful owners of green bucks printing machines persuaded the world to make this dollar as international currency. In this way we can cooperate, trade with many different countries and we don't have to take in count all individual exchange rates. We don't have to exchange one currency into another, predict exchange rates. We don't have to care if there are any needed goods in the country we are receiving currency for our goods. We just calculate the relation of the currency to the dollar. When Germen are selling goods in France they don't have to calculate how much Franks they get and what they could buy for those Franks in France. All trading recalculates all exchange rates to dollar and for the dollar anybody can buy almost anything in almost any country. It doesn't matter that all transactions are done in green dollars. The US was making wars in the Middle East and near Russia to keep control over oil. Later they forced Arabs to agreement that oil would be traded in green bucks only. After that all West World was happy.

Someone says that after stimulus there would be too much green dollars on the world market and the dollar would devaluate.

US import is larger than export then the dollars are going out of the country to the wide world. What is going on with them? Everybody (mayby except Russia) needs oil then they use those dollars to pay for oil. We think the Arabs are investing their received dollars and buying US T-bills. You could think they are buying US and US has obligation to pay back one day. The green buck is coming back home. T-Bills are not any special goods like oil, coffee, cars but just pieces of paper promising that after some time at maturity this piece of paper can be exchanged for more dollars. The Arabs are buying T-Bills and green buck is coming home. The printer's owners destroy it for now and amount of dollars on the world market is reduced. After the term or at proscribed times T-Bill's owner receives interest and fraction of dollars is going out on the market. At maturity T-Bill's owner gets what he paid plus interest. What the Arabs are doing with the bucks? Nothing, really. They don't need it because they keep receiving more greens for oil in continuos way. What the Arabs can do with the green for cashed T-Bills? They just buy more new T-Bills. The only influence on TBills and Dollar the Arabs have is reducing oil production and it is not that simple to do it. When part of the T-Bills is not reinvested in the new T-Bills the obligation has to be paid in dollars. The printer's owners don't care and US government cries there is no money to pay debts and the government grabs more taxes from taxpayers.

The question is what a government is doing with money. Government is collectiong taxes, pays for social services, transportation and few other things. Most of collected from tax payers money goes to defence system and technical advances what means military technology. Does anybody know how much of the defence money is reaching its destination? These are so incredibly huge amounts it is very easy to take lion's part away and destroy it and nobody will notice specially because all military industries are in the same hands of the owners of the money printers. Why the government is creating T-Bills? It should use the money to build roads, bridges and so on. Ok they built it or not. It is time for maturity of the T-Bills and where is the government taking money to pay it? Of course from the taxes. If it is so then money coming from issuing the new T-Bills could be taken out of circulation and when there is need to pay at the maturity tax payers money are used.

I think there is no need to keep destroying large amounts of the money. It just has to be kept the same amount in the circulation.

The world riches are buying gold. It is similar story. Gold mines owners are those who print money then part of the money received for gold can be destroyed too. Unlike common believes there is not many of gold bars all over the world. Most of it is in one safe. The safe is in Kentucky where for "small" fee gold is stored together with many kind of deseases, viruses, medicines and whatever terrible exists. They are on the territory of the biggest US military unit. Then again it all stays at home all the time.

I'm not sure if my thinking is close to the truth but if printing money would cause inflation we would be able to see it very often.

There is one more aspect. The world is growing. There is more and more production, consumption, and goods in the world what needs much more transactions. Some say there is no more money based on precious metals because we needed more and more of those metals. There is not enough precious metals in the world to cover all transactions. Some time ago the new gold in large amounts arrived to Europe and it made mess on the market. Right now the Earth has no more secrets and there is no hope to find much gold from new unknow yet sources. To help with the shortage we are using green bucks instead of gold. Growing world market needs more money what is OK and there is only need to keep correct balance.

For 60 years since WWII people as well as firms were always paying back debts plus interest. More money is coming back than going out from the banks. For all that time part of the money could be taken out of circulation little by little. As the proof we are seeing deflation from time to time. They say there is deflation going on in Japan for over 10 years and Japanese government has hard time to deal with it. Right now in US after the stimulus and after advertizing the stimulus as introduction more new money to the market the value of dollar has not dropped down and actually it went up a little bit. There must be some truth in what I'm saying.

There are talking about corrections on the stock exchanges and housing market. I think each stock exchange correction specially those causing recessions has the only purpose to remove money from the market and decrease inflation. When people own a lot of shares the riches like Mr. X have dollars. The correction is created and share prices are going down. At this point the riches can destroy part of the dollars. Later people need money and the riches are buying back shares paying low price. After while people keep working and earning then they are ready to buy shares again and share prices are driven up and people have to pay a lot to riches. When prices are high enough and enough money is taken from the people another correction is made every correction is causing the people, the small and medium firms and organizations are losing money. The riches can speculate money out from the people and take them of the circulation by destroying. The game starts from beginning.

An example with Warren Buffett.

I was always telling everybody that if the man from Omaha
would invest all money in tech stocks in nineties and sold
everything in December 1999 he would have so much money.
He could go to the Arabs and buy them all including all oil, all
countries, all sheiks with their wives and pay cash for it. It didn't
happen because Mr. Buffett is really nobody and he has to do
what he is told to do. He was told to do something else. Now
when he gave his cash for shredding he's got little worth shares.
It doesn't make any difference. He is so rich that if he would
lose 90% of what he owns he still would have more than he
could spend. After that he was waiting in peace until shares go
up and then he began selling it to the people. When cycle stop
going up the shares will drop down and excess of cash can be
destroyed. If Mr. Warren would buy high tech shares then many
of those firms don't exist anymore and he wouldn't be able to
sell shares and keep swinging stock market. Anyway no matter
what he does he can periodically give a lot of dollars for
destroying. The masters are planning to make full cycle and
keep control on the way up as well on the way down.

The ridicules nation from under the sign of maple leaf.

There is relation between US Dollar and Canadian Dollar. One side of it is when Canadian dollar is low the Americans can exchange small amount of their money and buy many Canadian stocks. On stock exchange in Toronto and other cities in Canada you have to trade in Candian Dollars. Later when Canadian dollar is stronger they can sell those share and exchange back to US dollar with high profit. The profit is high even when shares have the same price in Canadian dollars. Nothing has changed, the stocks are on the same level but masters took large amount of green dollars from Canada and they destroyed it. It is killing two birds with one arrow. The masters were holding controlling amount of shares in so called Canadian firms and they could force the firms to give favorable contracts or prices to American cooperators or customers. The masters dictate the price of oil produced on Canadian territory. Keeping control of this price they have big influence on world oil prices. All excess of dollars is removed from the circulation. Since in Canada there is very little of anything of Canadian industries the aspect described above is not that important. The most important is the oil price. When oil price is going up, Canadian dollar is going up because by "gentlemen agreement" owners of so called Canadian oil should not make more profit in Canada than in other parts of the world. To exhaust this subject we need to know that whatever is under the ground in Canada does not belong to Canada at all. Everybody can (and the American Masters already did) to just register land for exploration. Please pay attention not to buy the land but just to register for very little fee. All the sources are already in the hands of foreign mostly American hands. After registering they can come and destroy everything on the ground as long as it is at least 500 m from residences. Cottages don't count as residences and they could be leveled with the ground without informing cottage's owners.

What implication has a fact that American Dollar is not American at all.

If green buck were American it would be much more difficult to speculate and manipulate it. The congress could have something to say about it. When one party would like to take some control from the other party they would do audit and large sum of missing money could be detected. On the other hand the audit results depend on who is more powerful and can put stroner pressure on auditors. (It is the same with water in Ontario lake. When they check why the beaches are unsafe they find US fault and they wash out they hands.) Since the green buck is owned by about five private persons they can do whatever they want. They can print more, shread it, send it out to circulation and tak it back. Sometimes someone is raising voice. One day a senator from New England yelled at Greenspan that dollars are printed too much. The very next day someone attacked US diplomatic place in Asia. Change of subject. The senator was reprimanded and he will never dare to touch this subject again. The balance is correct because the country (what a stupid term country) is in debt with printer's owners and it is said every dollar taken out of circulation is for paying back the interest.

I do not favor any conspiration theories. I know wherever is about big money there are no accidents and every move is planned carefully. The planners are not the smartest brains in the world and from time to time it could turn the way they did not wanted. They have enough power to twist every situation to get benefits. The worse is when nothing is going on. When there is something going on it is easier to rock it and then push in desired direction.

For example lotteries and casinos. The fact is the jackpot is going to accidental people but lately there was a lot of noise about selling tickets lottery machine renters. They were winning few or tens of thousand dollars every few weeks. It is statistically impossible. It was not a one time winning but every few weeks a little bit.

In theory T-Bills are issued to cover government expenses for people. They are because they usually were paid back at maturity. When congress was warried how to pay the dollar printers purchased a lot of T-Bills. It is rubbish. It looks like they paid themselves. No it is not. Right now the government is deeper in debts. In America we are brainwash about the law and everybody can sue everybody. Congressmen are quiet or printers will sue for paying debts. Case closed. It would be so easy to take printing rights from the printers and give it back to congress. Most debts would disappeare in a moment.

The world is in debt with dollar printers.

The comedians don't have to be jocking how it is the all countries are in debt and where? It is clear they are in debt with printing money machines owners.

The Russia is still strong. They never needed banks because machine guns could send people to work any time. It is changing out there and I hope the Russia is not getting weaker. Russia wants to build pipeline to India and China. To prevent it there is constant war in Afghanistan. Iran wanted to create a bursa and sell oil in euro or rubels then army went to search nuclear weapons in Iran. There are demonstrations and killing heads of states wherever are goods like in Lybia. It is all to prevent oil free market.

Eurpean Union was created just to make one printing money center.

Some countries want independends then their government is exchnaged for anothers. They killed Polish government in plane crash. Greece and Italy are changing peacefully.

Polish situation.

There isn't neither a lot of money nor stocks nor mines nor factories in Poland then there is no need to manipulate stock exchanges or house market. The whole sum can be twisted in a week.

After the WWII they changed money. They paid 1 new zl for 100 old zl but in workplaces they were exchanging 100 old zl for 3 new zl. It seams to not matter if you have 100 old zl or 1 new zl. It is not the same thing because you could exchange in bank 20,000 only. Whoever had more lost it all. People were looking for poor friends to ask them to go to the bank and exchange money. The experiences made poles preffering to keep money in pillows than in banks. The Polish currency didn't matter and people had to hold on to dollars or real estates.

This is the reason the recession in Poland is not like anywhere else.

America in debt with China

All media feeding us with opinions but decades of experience tells us that main purpose of the media is not to inform people but to brainwash people and push untrue views into our minds. We can safely assume when media are telling too loud something it is always about something else.

One of the latest view is USA is in debt with Chinese. I want to figure out how it really is.

If a country would be like a corporation then it would be possible to issue shares to get money. When in Chinese hands would land significant number of shares (not necessary 51%) they would start to take control. The country do not have share and in theory the control is in puppets sanators and other authorities.

How US is getting in debts? Usually the government issues T-Bills and government's bonds. To make it simple lets assume the bonds and T-Bills are like the same thing. The main difference is the term to maturity and the bonds could pay some interest before the maturity.

What is such a bond and how it works?

Let's say the American government issues one bond. Someone actually anyone brings $700 and gives it to the government. For that sum receives a piece of paper. The paper is promising the government will pay back to the owner of the paper $1000 in 10 years (or 15 years or..). At the time of receiving the bond $700 is the price of TV in US or it covers 4 years of salary for average worker in China. I say 4 years because it was the case in Poland where monthly salary was $10-$15.

What is the bond value right after the issue date? ZERO!

What is the bond value 7 years later or 9 years later? ZERO!

The piece of paper has no value before maturity. 10 years later at the maturity it has value $1000 paid by the government.

Does US government care if the $700 brought American or Chinese? Not at all. The $700 is the $700. Ok, what will happen 10 years later at the maturity? Nobody knows but the inflation could go up and at this day TV will cost $1100. What then? In such case the American will not be able to buy TV for money received for the bond. In other case scenario when exchange rate in China is changed $1000 could cover one month salary only. I'm saying one month because it did happen in Poland.

I don't understand what could be wrong with bonds sold to Chinese investments. Whoever brings dollars gives dollars now. There was no running inflation in US yet but it could happen. The inflation could just grow faster. Every inflation helps those who issued bonds because at maturity they will pay promised amount of dollars although less valuable amount. In theory the gain on bond should cover inflation and give some additional interest but you never know. In case of China we can safely assume the exchange rate of they currency will change sooner or later.

With all loans is like in an old Greek joke. Icshak was worried because he borrowed a lot of money from Moshe and he was not able to pay it back on time. After few days he went somewhere, came back home relaxed and happy. His wife asks where did you go and what changed your mood? Icshak answers "I told Moshe I don't have money and now Moshe has to worry about it".

Ok, that's generally all. There are secondary aspects. If happens that Chinese will get really a lot of bonds they will receive a lot of dollars at maturity. What could they buy for dollars? It would be different story with a country whose currency would be in other country people's hands. There is less trouble with dollars because green bucks are not American Dollars and they have little to do with US. It is an international currency. In this case the Chinese can buy goods all over the world and little just in US. They could buy oil mostly. When in 10 years oil price goes up the Chinese is losing because one could buy less oil for $1000 than 10 years earlier for $700.

When Chinese would have more dollars than they need for oil they would be forced to keep buying American products in US. Having demands on the market American businesses would expand and increase production what is good for the country. Sure it could drive prices higher but masters don't care. We the people would pay the higher price and they would have larger profits.

Someone could argue that Chinese having a lot of dollars could start buying shares of American companies. No worry. They are not stupid. They know shares have no value in themselves and nobody seles to public enough shares to lose controlling number.

If this would happen then at first American factories start producing more. When production grows slower than demands the prices are going up. When prices are going up inflation is growing. When inflation is higher Chinese can buy less for $1000 now than for $700 ten years earlier and Chinese are losing. Anyway dollars will come to American factories helping industry to grow.

After crossing critical point when there is few American goods to buy and Chinese have a lot of money they could panic and start paying more and more for the goods and growing inflation will make them lose more and more. If they don't panic and demand grows in controlled way it could be negative for American people because the prices would grow faster than salaries. If the masters of America can still keep control they will increase salaries. In any above described scenario people who live from day to day from a paycheck to the next paycheck will not see much difference. Chinese would lose more or less anyway.

No matter how one would look at the scenarios the Chinese are not any danger for US.

As conclusion from the previous consideration we know that main purpose of the stock exchanges is to create correction, recessions to suck money out of the market from general population and businesses. The money is destroyed decreasing inflation. On the other hand when Chinese buy a lot of shares of many corporations or plenty of shares of one corporation it means nothing. As we know only the controlling amount of shares counts. The true owners always hold controlling number of shares for themselves and the remaining shares are used to speculate on stock exchange. Whatever is going on with those shares the corporation owners never really cares The fact is the directors sometimes are selling their share but it is happening only when the firm is going down and they want to grab something for themselves in last minute. To prevent it there is a rule stating the directors have to inform public when they are selling or buying shares.

I think all those Chinese, Arabs and whoever buying US government bonds are doing it only because they have spare money and cannot do anything else with it. Keeping all cash in a pillow one loses because of inflation. Average folks are buying CDs because it is guaranted and the interest is guaranted. When someone belives the inflation is lower than CD's interest and has nothing else in mind then one buys CDs. CDs are usually in one piece and it would be suspitious to bring million dollars to a bank and to buy 200 of the same CDs $5000 each. When one buys papers like bonds they could be split easily. In addition the swindlers invented trading bonds before maturity then those worthless pieces of paper can be sold before maturity when you find someone more stupid who would buy it. The fake value is unsure and it depends on other things on the market but one can sell it somehow anyway. Chinese or Arabs are buying American government bonds instead of Greek bonds means they are hoping the better or worse could happen but US will survive and the government would pay on maturity. It isn't that sure since not so long ago banks began fake bankruptcy and the financial media suggested buying T-Bills because they are the most guaranted and possible to cash. It was only pushing crowd to buy T-Bills and between the lines message told us the government papers could be as worthless at maturity as other things.

I don't believe US could just go bankrupt and will survive the bad times too. The problem with US industry is there was no war since the Civil War and country could grow in peace and the growth was driven by wars in the other parts of the world providing military goods. There was no real war since WWII and other countries have been growing too. Since the other countries are not on isolated islands like US their products unlike the American products were improving.

Whatever we say it is Orwell's fault. All actions in last decades want to burn the number on every person like on cows and send everybody to work. Computers will be able to alter everyones health, wealth and criminal records. The only thing to take care is to scare people to make sure there are no uprisings.

The land value.

The real value of the land.

The land was always needed by people but it always has very little value.

The value of the land is little because whatever grows by itself has very little necessary nutritions for people. Most free growing plants are weeds, trees not giving fruits and bushes. Animals are not able to change anything in their environment then they have to somhow somewhere find food. Sure some animals like bevers can change environment and make better habitats. As for food most animals have to be content with whatever grows by itself but they don't eat whatever green is around. They pick special plants or part of the plants like leaves, fruits, grass blades. People are more sophisticated and for higher physical and intellectual activities higher nutritions are needed.

People find special plants they want to eat. The value of the land is low because only for about 3 years one can grow the same plant good enough for food. After another 2 maybe three years all minerals are used and no new plants can grow anymore. A little help was to change plants and for the fourth and fifth year grow something else what needs a bit different minerals from the soil but after that is the end of farming anyway. Sure, there were special cases like Nil river flooding annually and bringing new nutritions for plant. In most cases people were trying to help by burning large land areas and in this place they could start growing food again. Useless pieces of unfertile lands were covering with weeds in time and after couple of years all could be burned again and farming would start from beginning.

On the other hand whatever the land is the food is not growing by itself. People have to work hard on farms. We see the most benefits are from the hard work of human and very little just form the land. For example the rice farms required enormous amount of work and the work has to be done accurately and with exact temperature, humidity, watering, amount of sunshine and perfect timing.

There were times when people believed in great land values. It was because when land was owned by few and others were working on farms as slaves or very little paid workers. The salaries were in small amount of food only. Every slave and slave like worker believed that if they were the land owners they would have wounderful rich lives. After some time the land owners began giving pieces of land to those who work on it as a payment for work. It turned out it wasn't so great after all. In reality the new land is giving the most food production. After years no matter what you do the soil is not fertile anymore and nobody can grow any food there. At those times after working hard for very little payment whoever worked on the same piece of land for ten or fifteen years received ownership to the land. They were giving the land mostly because it was not fertile at all. Those new little land owners instead to become rich and happy with plenty of food had to keep working for the large land owners and only in a free time trying to grow something on the new land they owned. The newly received pieces of land were unable to grow almost anything.

In Poland at the end of XIX century and in the first half of the XX century the land seamed to be a treasure because there were families with many children who had to live farming own small pieces of land. At that time there was almost no possibility to have any other profession than farmers. When one family had larger farm than others they were portrayed as riches because they had enough food to eat. All others assumed the very high value of the land. Additional and misleading factor was political situation. People couldn't live peacefully to farm the land until the land lost all fertility. The two world wars destroyed housing, all belonging and killed grand numbers of people. Everybody was thinking that owning large amount of lands would give them wealth and happiness. The wars were not in every country in the world and life showed the land cannot produce enough food anyway.

People have to spend a lot of time and use a lot of components to produce agricultural tools and machines in order to make farming useful and giving resonable production. Unfertile soil requires from people plenty of unnatural work to produce fertilizers necessary to make enough food to grow. Edible plants are prone to deseases, more extreme climate changes and invasive pests. And again we see that all the additional work to create artificial conditions necessary and desired by food production is more important than soil by itself. In the next step produced food very often have to be transported to very distant destination what requies food modification to extend natural expiration dates.

Land as investment

We have the land value and more often in common understanding we talk about the price of the smaller or larger land areas. From economic point of view the land just as the land has very little value. Land value is very often mistaken as the value of the real estate on the land.

Investing in the land is almost always the worse kind of investment.

Yes, it happens that very inexpensive useless piece of land is expensive after 20 or 50 years but it does not mean anyone is making a lot of money on it. There is very few people in the world who have plenty of spare money to buy useless piece of land wait 20 or 30 years and sell it well. Most average people who own useless piece of land which gains value have to wait much loger time. Taking in count inflation and what the same money invested somewhere else could do we see the land price would have to grew 3 or 4 times more than it did to give the same profit.

Yes, there are people called builders-developers who are portrayed as those who make money on the land but it is not entire truth. Firstly average folks buying the same useless piece of land would never new if or when the price in this area goes up. When there is hope or rumor that prices of useless pieces of land are going to go up the builders are already buying or owning it and common folks would have to pay already inflated prices what would bring very limited profit or no profit at all.

What is done to increase the land prices?

In reality the developer never makes money on land pieces. Buying, owning and selling pieces of land is part of their business because they buid buildings on pieces of land. In this line of work they do not make money on land but when they all land transaction do timely they minimize loses on land. The builders do it in following way: they buy inexpensive large pieces of land and later using all tricks like bribery, corruption, conspiration, blackmailing they force local and sometimes higher level government people to change the law, by-law, zoning, development plans to set the land owned by the builders as primary location for development. In this case the pure value of land is not going up much but comparing empty land to the same land 30 years later when it is part of a new subdivision the price is up a lot. Sometimes there are single lots between newly created subdivisions. The price of such piece is up but not as much as similar piece with a new house on it. The reason is that building a single house costs much more than building one of the many houses in the same subdivision. The price for building such a single house goes additionally up because the future owner spends a lot on tiny details important for him but difficult to make it happed. The next future owner of the same house would never be interested in those details at all. The owner of the single lot is wasting so much money that the whole investment is losing its purpose and decreasing significantly gain on the land value.

There was a special case in Poland during the last two decades where the real estate value went up a lot. I think the real reson was changing exchange rate of polish zloty to American dollar.

Dalai Lama

We all need something bigger and better than reality.

Young people are open on all events in the world and they believe they can change the world and build better future for everybody.

Part of the young generation have good talents. Very often they go to colleges and universities. They learn there new things. Horizons are opening in front of them and because they have no baggage of bad life experiences they reach interesting conclusions on various subjects. The conclusions are often completely different than commonly accepted wisdom.

It is the same in USA. The young people in universities and colleges are full of energy. They see what's wrong in society, politics, economy and natural environment.

For unspringing energy many young people in universities are gathering in groups under various names and reasons. They go on demonstrations.

Such activities are totally useless because nobody pays any attention to them and they usually demonstrate peacefully. Those behaviors could be and are used.

It is easy to artificially increase tension, change direction and use students energy to own purpose. Watching those demonstrators it is easy to find who will always follow like a sheep, who could be a leader and who is hard to be manipulated. There is no danger that demonstration could get out of control. At any time provocation can be made, police gets in to action following the arrests of those more active who are asking inconvenient questions. Fixed court and sentences leave records and cross out whole future lives.

Big part of young population is too lazy to to do anything or they realized they are powerless and they give up any public activities. The smarter and stronger start using their energy to increase skills, get professional knowledge to make the easier life for themselves.

Many young people fall into apathy and oblivion. They spend a lot of time in clubs drinking, taking drugs. The most sensitive with the best meaning (best meaning in this world means weaker) young people begin taking interest in cults, unknown religions or whatever new and exotic they can find. They go after unknown and exotic because they hope there is something good somewhere out there.

Getting interested in exotic philosophy.

Exotic is always attractive and large crowd of young people is passing by places where someone is telling completely different opinions about anything. Commercial America is watching carefully where young people are and what they are interested in. Following them and shaping their opinions and interests provides market needs for near future years. Those young people are always the target audience.

Young and not destroyed yet are sensitive to unjustice. When something bad is happening to anybody in the world the young people feel compation, they want to help and they are interested in this subject.

When youth starts focusing on unjustice, obuse, terrorizing done by American businesses the whole thing is played low and gets quiet. When youth focus is on cases favored by American business then everything is blown out of proportion to the point the average folks lose understanding what reality is. By the way new products supporting such view are on the market.

China has huge population and everybody is kept in strong hand. Any industrial, economic, technological grow is controlled, stimulated and financed from outside. There is always possibility that Chinese could uprise and create armed opposition.

Somewhere up in the highest Himalayas Mountain in Tybet exsists tiny about 1000 people group. They would preffer to be independent from China. They don't count at all because their population is so tiny, they don't have any neither industrial nor intellectual power at all and there is nothing interesting under the ground of their territory. They have a leader Dalai Lama. Seams nothing but they could be useful for Americans in case China starts acting on they own or they would began any industrial or economic activities without American's approval. Provocation would be made and American army could attack China for pretended help for Tybet.

When or if we can hear anything about Tybet it means that agreed and approved version is in the media crying how Chinese violated Tybetans human rights.

Adopting philosophy to business.

When American business noticed youth is focusing on Tybet they already blew up the whole story about independence and high intellect Tybetans. Many monks, mostly fake monks were imported to US and they were telling prepared stories. At the same time monks and few people around them began wearing the same style clothes. One of the products was Hush Puppies shoes. It saved the Hush Puppies brand from bankruptcy.

Dalai Lama wisdom and purpose of his existence.

On the wave of commercials swam up Dalai Lama who slowly became famous known at least by his name in the whole world. Who is Dalai Lama? Nobody, really. A leader of group population around 1000 who lives somewhere up in the mountain. There are many Pacific islands with population around 1000 and nobody knows they exist. We don't have to look any farther. In Canada the chief of the First Nation is the leader of much more people and nobody cares about them, Canadian government doesn't care and takes lands where they live, evicts them, takes their children and gives them for adoption to strange families or accidentally or on purpose doesn't purifies they drinking water.

Dalai Lama is very special because American psychologists, sociologists write books for him. He is celebrated all over the world like someone significant. In reality it is just artificially kept alive reason for future military attack on China.

Business.

My business

My business was an international corporation then from legal, taxation and accounting point of view everything had to be done the same way as all very large international businesses are doing.

It was not a business at all in common understanding of what business is. The agent was finding one by one contracts for me. In common meaning business is something what is buying, selling, producing something. Such businesses have many fixed assets buildings, machines, equipment which you could see and touch. In my business all assets was just intellectual property meaning my knowledge and skills.

Starving business.

The first kind of business is very poor. Someone registers it and from time to time performs small tasks like mowing the lawn, fixing plumbing, small home repairs. Most activities to forging books and avoiding to pay any taxes. Usualy it passes unnoticed because it is not worth to spend time on auditing.

Very small business on the verge of surviving.

The next business to small variety store or service. It is very often family business. When woman in the family has no job she can be saleswoman in this store. They don't make much or any profit at all but if it is a grocery store and the family gets free food from it then business is good enough. They cheat, lie and forge documentation and by hiring all family members including adolescnet ones they avoid paying taxes. The owner has to worry where to find and how to buy the least expensive product to be sold for a bit higher price.

Business with profit.

Another type of business is the one bringing a profit. Usualy activities start in the way that a worker while working for someone is trying to keep good relation with customers and in time quits the job and starts doing the same service on his own stealing cutomers from his former boss. Later such a business stabilizes on the market but the main concern is always fighting with competitors, blocking own employees from performing task on they own and stealing customers from the competition. Most payments is done in cash and this way lets avoid paying taxes. Important is to stay under the radar, never catch anybody's attention otherwise someone could get interested in, cause auditing and detect all fraudulent actions. This kind of business pays very little taxes if pays at all.

Regular working business.

Average kind of business is stabilized on the market, has determined number of customers, gives profit and pays taxes. Activities could be split in following way. The 10% for performing tasks what the business suppose to do. The 30% watching and fighting with competitors. To have profits at least 50% of activities has to be done with customers who don't pay with own money. The rest 10% is disappearing in the background to make sure the business is not catching anybody's eye.

Finding customers who don't pay with own money means that service is paid by insurance. Car body shop makes the most by reapiring insured cars from accidents. Car owner doesn't care how expensive the repair is. Another and the most popular is to make services for the city, province and partly warranty services. It is extremely important not to step on anybody's toe and keep sweet relation with government offices.

Large business.

A large business is the business which has very large profits and is moving very large sums of money. I will explain it on an example of a builder-developer. The fact building, construction is not much of importance. Actual construction work requires to find someone who will coordinate works, hire subcontractors and will not steal from nor cheat on the business owner. The developer's activities begin with finding right land for development. After buying this land the developer has to bribe, persuade, blackmail key people in the local governmet to direct planning department to assign the land for development and to receive most of necessary permits as well as exclusive rights for this development. After that the developer bribes, persuades local real estate agents who will advertise this land as great location what let's driving house prices up. During all the constructions and selling the developer has to feed pockets of many more significant people in area to make them closing eyes on all more or less legal moves.

Usually developer should pay development fee what is kind of tax from every built house. In this case the developer goes into agreement with local authorities that instead of really paying developers fee to the town he will build roads or school. For example when developers suppose to pay 2 million dollars and cost of building a school is slightly below 2 million dollars the developers gets contract to build a school costing 4 million dollars. The 2 million would be what he suppose to pay as developers fee and another 2 millions he will receive from the town. In this manner building the school doesn't cost him anything and actually he makes minimal profit on it. He does not pay any developers fee either. This developer keeps close relation with local authorities because he puts a lot of money in their pockets and at the same time he keeps all details and bribery proofs. This is his guarantee nobody would ever dare to dig out details.

This builder will have easier way for future developments and will always receive more favorable deals than others. In the future such developer can get contract to build two washrooms for $800,000. Everybody is happy. Local authorities don't care how much it costs town it is property tax payers not their own money. The builder makes huge profits and hard working people just pay more and more taxes because the people have no say on any subject anyway. By the way of conducting this kind of business the developer has to have such good relation with local authorities that they would not allow any kind of auditing.

Large scale domestic business.

Every large scale domestic business it is just pure criminal activities.

Creating and activities a large scale business has nothing to do with any work done. The owners of such a business don't have and don't need any technical knowledge and actually any such knowledge would stay in the way of doing it. For example anybody knowing anything about solar panels knows it has no economical sense and would have very hard time to do solar panel business in spite of this knowledge. Producing electric cars is useless because there is not enough electrical energy in the world to cover 10% of its need. If we today start building nuclear power stations like crazy (I'm not saying that we should or it is save or how expensive it would be) and connecting them to the grid then after about 30 years we could achieve the level considered as necessary for electric cars. Additional condition would be any other electricity demands stay on today's level. The same story is about hydrogen cars. Every advertisement says we have plenty of hydrogen in the water what is true. Unfortunately splitting molecules of water into hydrogen and oxygen uses much more energy than we can get from hydrogen fuel. It is obvious that hydrogen for fuel will never come from splitting water.

The domain in which the business will be active depends only on what kind and were connected powerful people the business owner is associated with.

At first the owner of the future business persuades or better yet gives orders to the government to set needed law. Later it tells government to take tax payers money and use it to do work preparation for the business. It could be building train track, roads, airports, do geological research etc. For example GM never produced any hybrid car. They've just put "Hybrid" sign on regular Malibu to get government fincning. The business works the best if it is organized as cartel what means or works related to produce components from beginning to the final so called product at the very end is in one hand. This way when the business owner wants to make money on building train tracks the government gives contracts for building tracks. When the business is building airports then the government orders building many new airports regardless if they are needed or not.

For deeper understanding how such large business works let's take an example from solar panel electricity generation business.

At first the future business owner tells government to make a law that every kWh produced by solar panels will be paid twice as much as from other generators and that when solar panel business needs electricity like in the night they will pay for every kWh half what anybody else is paying. It is good enough and the business owner can put a fence around large land area and mark it as private property with severe penalty for trespassing. In the center put one solar cell from a calculator. Connect one cable to the electrical grid and on the other side fenced area cable from the grid. When the business owner connects those to cables together he makes 4 times profit on every kWh passing through the fenced area. Oh, one more thing. The owner must forbid government any kind of auditing. Very large scale business is ready. There could be done some more. The business owner tells government to make a law that solar panel business doesn't pay any taxes. It is possible to do more. One of the firm in the cartel could produce solar panels. Since such production is economically impossible than the business owner tells government to steal taxes and finance all solar panel production. Panels are sold with profit to the solar panel generation station. Profit is taken by the owner and government pays for the panels before they are fake used inside the fenced land. Sure someone could figure out what is going on using Google Earth or any other satellite images than government is buying all satellite images from all satellites.

Law is the law then someone else could try to do the same creating competition. There is another law created and special commission giving licenses to produce and to use solar panels. Of course nobody else will ever get such a license. It is not called a monopoly because in theory someone could get the license. Just in case there is a need to introduce some kind of "carbon tax" to give breaks for our businessman and penalize all others.

Great American international scale businesess.

It is very simple. All activities are running in cycles.

We start from any point in the cycle.

The grand businessman has factories in America but they are getting outdated and already almost don't bring any profit.

The businessman tells the president to give money to any ter ro rystic organization like C ia and send them to find somewhere in the world a place where would be anything desirable like coal, oil, nikel, diamonds, uranium under the ground and it would be in strategic geographical position. Later this hired organization finds any two slightly antagonistic groups of people. The businessman tells the president to give the organization money for Russian machine guns, tanks and all kind of military equipment and give it to the both antagonistic group. Later the organization decides which group would be more dependant on helpers and do whatever they will be told to do. The organization feeds them with ideology and is causing the war. The more dependant group will win the war and as thanks to the sponsors the leaders will sign agreement with our businessman to do whatever he wants to do.

When war is doing its damages the businessman tells the president to send army for keeping peace. In a mean time there is alredy decided who wins the war and who will be a puppet leader in their country.

The army needs equipment then the businessman takes more money from the president to produce the equipment. He takes lion's part for himself, uses part for finacing for all kind of technical (electronics, biology, chemical) experiments. You know he wouldn't waste own money on such things. When any experiments turns well all profits are going to the businessman pocket. The rest of the president's money is really used on military production.

The war in the distant country is kept alive for as long as possible because it makes improvements to the businessman factories and factories during such war and after have to bring profits.

At one point the people in the distant country don't want to fight with each other regardless how much money they receive from the president. Then and only then a new government is set with the puppet leaders.

Right after this war in a distant country the businessman tells the president to give money for restoring destroyed country. The money is not going to anybody in such country anyway. The businessman is going to such country and gets untermed and unconditional agreement to explore underground anything he wants and to build any kind of factories, refineries he wants with guarantee that no tax ever would be paid. The business takes money from the president some equipment and specialists from own factories in US and goes to the distant country. The war is over and nobody needs any goods produced by businessman's factories located in US. Everything is paid by the presinet.

The businessman just has to make sure that any kind of production in the distant country is not independent and requires heavy cooperation with counterparts located on US soil.

After a couple of years everything is built and installed what needed to be and factories, mines, refineries are working well and bringing good profit. All profits are going to the businessman pocket. He does not improve anything, he does not upgrade anything he does not modernize anything because it costs money and something valuable would be in foreign land.

After another couple of years all our businessman's factories are getting outdated, require general maintenance and stop bringing high profit. The business cycle is closed.

The cycle starts from the beginning..

Anybody asks where the president is taking money form?

The first part from our taxes and later?

It is so simple. The businessman is the owner of green bucks printing machines. I'm assuming that by this time everybody knows the dollars and printing machines are in private hands and have nothing to do with US government. Landing freshly printed money has additional effect. In case the president would ever try to stand up against the businessman then he will be asked to pay back debts and whole thing is quiet.

The presidents are changing and this is not a new story. Why the president is getting involved in such machinations? He is a puppet president like all others.

"Modern" technologies.

Electric car

According to real technical data published by one of the electric car manufacturer one charge requires about twice as electricity as an average household in 24 hours. With real or slightly exaggerated single charge car driving distance one needs to charge each car at least once a day. We can assume there are on average two cars per household.

2 X 2 + 1=5 Two cars twice electricity plus the household means that we would need 5 times of electricity we are using today.

To provide so much electricity we would have to start building nuclear power stations like crazy, we would not be allowed to increase any other electricity needs and after about 30 years we would achieve enough to charge our electric cars.

The bumper invented by Mr. Lucjan Lagiewka.

Mr. Lucjan Lagiewka haven't graduated from any university and is an inventor who is working on kinetic energy. He says that Newton's law is true in case of two objects participating in collision. When there are three or more objects the physical law is different. I believe that physical law is the same regardless how many objects are involved. In case of multi object collision everything is just much more complicated.

In case of two objects everything is easily understandable but when we have additional objects changing linear motion into rotation the calculations are really complicated. In simply explanation taking example of a bumper we know the objects are hard solid. The car and obstacle are solid hard. The result of collision and slowing down depend on amount of changing speed in considered time of the incident. When car driving 100 km/h start braking and go to full stop in 15 secunds passengers almost don't feel any rapid stopping. When in another case the car collides with a solid obstacle and stops motion in 0.1 seconds than passengers and all things in the car will feel very rapid shock and people could die from it. In a car with Mr Lagiewka's bumber there is additional equipment with large mass which can rotate. The bumper is connected to this device where linear movement is changed into circular movement. It is similar to 4-cycle gasoline engines where linear movement of the piston is changed into circular motion of the transmission. Pressing the bumper we are changing its linear motion into circular motion of the large mass in the device. When the mass and its movement is calculated correctly most of the impact energy is turning into rotary motion in the device and only small amount effects the rest of the car including passengers and goods.

It is not truth that the device is absorbing or dissolving energy and impact cannot be felt inside the car. The thing is the in case of the car without the bumper invented by Mr. Lagiewka whole change of speed to full stop takes let's say 0.1 second. In case the car has Mr. Lagiewka's device impact is in large part going into changing linear motion into circular motion in the device and much smaller part is causing slowing the car down. When the whole incident takes about 1 second than passengers feel everything in much less rapid way.

The car manufacturers are not interested in Mr. Lagiweka's device because real accidents proof the impacts could come from all possible directions and are very complicated. To protect passenger in real accidents would be very difficult end extremely expensive with compare to currently produced bumpers. The cars are not often bumpimg head on each other. All bumpers in all cars and all obstacles in the world would have to be on the same level above the ground. Since impact could be from any direction the devices would have to be all around the car. The car would look like a ball what is more funny than the cars in amusement park. In addition any impact not perpendicular to the bumper with this device splits into component forces and the Mr. Lagiewka's bumper would protect from the fraction of perpendicular force only.

As long as our cars don't look like billard balls where everywhere on every side and direction is installed Mr.

Lagievka's bumper that long we can't benefit from the invention.

Perpetuum Mobile

The difficulty to create perpetuum mobile is not that it is impossible to do it.

Nobody cares for real perpetuum mobile. All inventors want to create a machine working all the time and using free available energy. Nobody would ever sponsor such creators because their product neither would generate any profits in return nor provide any power for restricting its usage.

Children's education.

Definition of the terms for our common language.

There are children challenged in some way and they need a lot of help from their parents because they cannot learn prescribed school material by themselves.

There are very talented (I don't know what it really means) children who achieve success in spite of lack of any help from parents, teachers and without catching many fortunate events.

The success is always relative. For one woman the success is stabilized job, healthy family and children without major problems. For another person the success is constant long hours work in a lab what after many years leads to discovery and Nobel's prize. For someone else who most likely could receive the Nobel prize too the success is working out comfortable life and then doing something maybe useless but what is giving a lot of pleasure.

There is always a lot of talk about so called born with intelligence. In US there is an idiotic IQ. The IQ is idiotic because when two different people answers correctly the same number of questions they receive different IQ numbers. Anyone can in two weeks get prepared for IQ test and receive score at least 10 points higher. What kind of intelligence test it is when one can learn in two weeks. Statistics say people with very high IQ never achieve anything special in their life. In my opinion IQ test is only about street smart and showing off when one gets high score.

The intelligence is an ability to manipulate others. Lies, frauds, persuading, using all tricks to get the result.

Fortunate and unfortunate events

We say very often someone was lucky in this or that point in life. We say that fortunate accident pushed someone in good direction.

Most of such chances are not random. In life of everybody there are stages, situations and decisions making very big difference in the future life. The person needs to know about it and react in time and in way to get the most benefits from the situation. There are random good opportunity coming to everybody and the person has to recognize it and be prepared to not miss the good fortune.

In human activities common calendar has very important influence. Most actions start every year at the same point in calendar. Children always begin the new school year in fall. Opennings for all kind of courses, trainings are always at the same point in calendar. Not all children have the same chance because of the calendar. In the same class primary school are children who were born in the same calendar year. It is a huge difference whether the child was born in January or December of the same year. The child born in December is actually one year younger, physically weaker and intellectually less matured. It doesn't matter if someone is 45 or 44 years old but It matter the most when children are younger. The youngest child has very little chanse to achieve any success because the child will always be compared to the older children. The oldest child in the group has the easier life and it could cause that after short while the child will start working less and keep getting behind of own abilities and lose age advantage. The parents and teachers should pay attention and make sure the older children are working, learning enough to keep advancing.

In everybody's life there are days when the person is evaluated. It is extremely important to be in the best condition on such day.

Real life example.

Our friends' son was from the youngest age very talented pianist. There is annual competition in US for the young pianists. Of course the oldest child in the age bracket has the biggest chance to win it because this child was learning how to play piano about 20% to 30% longer than the youngest one. The parents and the teacher of our pianist sent him to the competition at the right time. The boy had great chances to win. The parents and the teacher knew the skills of couple of other competitors and believed that their son would get the first or the second place. For the finals each of the two boys suppose to play one last piece. In situation like that there were two pieces to choose from. One the most difficult one and play it well or the other less difficult and play it excellent. The decision was in the hands of the teacher and the parents. They picked the less difficult one and the boy played it in really excellent way. During the finals the other competitor picked the most difficult piece of music and played it all right. As I was told the other boy was not as good pianist as our friend's son. The first prize was given to the other competitor mostly because he played the most difficult piece of music. Was our talented artist worse? Some said he was better but decision picking the music to be played at the final caused him to get just the second place.

Primary school.

The advances in learning, successes or problems of students in a primary school depend on their parents in the most significant way.

The parents could be very educated or not. The parents could teach their children school subjects at home or not. It is not that important. The most important is to teach the child that there is a value in education and make the child to believe the knowledge is enriching lives. The next thing is to organize child's time in such way there is enough peaceful, without stress or distraction time for learning required school materials.

In my primary school time the scores depended mostly on who the child's parents were. When the parents were well connected their children for the same results were receiving better grades than the children's of nobody specials. It is because any teacher to prove own work needs to differentiate students scores and because he has to kiss more important people asses and their children scores are rounded up. To give someone worse scores the teacher chooses vulnerable children who's parents don't stand up to fight for justice. When poor child starts to fight against unjustice the teacher will never admits neither own fault nor unjustice. Worse comes to worst and the teacher hates the unjustly treated child as defense mechanism. From now on the teacher is looking forward to find any reason to punish unconvenient children.

The differences from unjust scores make almost as big difference as talent, systematic learning.

Of course in every class as in every community there are more talented students who advance in learning faster, easier and other students with some degree of difficulty in learning. When the students want to just disappear in tha background to avoid any trouble they can became the averagers regardless whom are their parents.

In every class there is one or more students who want to achieve good grades by licking behinds of the teachers and spying, ratting on other students. Almost all teachers (exception are few from the movies because the movie is just a fiction) like those traders because received from them information about other students gives the teacher additional leverage in controlling the class.

When less talented students with more important parents have some difficulty in learning the teachers are willing to spend extra time, give extra attention to help them. When nobody's child or less liked by teacher child needs help nobody cares. The teachers don't help such children just to show "who's the boss".

On the other side when children are good students and have important parents (Usually good students don't kiss asses of teachers and don't rat on others because they don't need to) the teachers do what they can to prize those children, send them as representants of the class or school or to any places where children could advance their skills.

Very good students with nobody parents don't receive any additional encouragement or help from the teachers and very often is discriminated. This situation is very difficult for the children because in addition to learning all school materials like all others and maybe involvement in after school activities these students have to fight with discrimination too. In such cases when those children deserve to be sent for competitions or for additional courses it is all denied for them and someone else is sent. It is heavy for those children and after years could be the major problem in the emotional growth.

Described above cases prove how important is the parent's role in children education.

The parents should pay attention and when their children have some difficulties in learning they should assign them more time for learning. Thanks that the students will keep skills in par with others. In case of more talented children the parents should make sure the children are not sitting on lauras but they enrich they knowledge.

It seams the positions and statuses of the parents cannot be changed but there is a work around. On one hand poorly set parents have no influence on the teachers and the school. On the other hand every parent can do a lot. Keeping close connection between parents and teachers could decrease antygonizing. In case of real unjustice the parent should take the student and immediately go to the teacher for a talk. Before going to school the parent has to be very well prepared to make sure he never ever throws untrue accusations. When during the conversation it does not look like the teacher understood own mistake and is not going to change wrong behavior the father should take control in his own hands. Regardless what the father social position is they have the same power. Less important fathers words will have more power. The parent should explain that he doesn't want better treatment or better scores than his child deserves but he will not allow for discrimination. The father should tell the teacher in one on one conversation that if the teacher dares to do any unjustice one more time than the parent will come and break the teacher's bones and any involving authority will cause as severe punishment as teacher's action deserves.

The father does not need to really ever do it but setting the problem and actions this way he will force the most arrogant, ignorant, unethical teacher to think over his own behavior.

Described above action is very controversial and most of the readers who never met much unjustice will not agree with me. I know it is right from my own experience. I had similar conversation with my teacher who wanted to do damage to my school grades. I knew his reasons not related to the school at all and I think he didn't know that I knew. The teacher was doing it only on the third party request. I was not a bandit and I would not keep my words for sure but the most important is from this point on the teacher treated me like an average other student and it made me satisfied.

The parents should watch when special, more significant day in the student's time is coming. When the children are evaluated somehow, when they have tests or exams the parents need to make sure the students are at their best.

On the other hand all children's successes or lack of them have a reason. What they learn in primary school is very generic shallow but everybody has better understanding in one than in another subject. The parents should remember they are excelling in one domain but it does not mean their children have any talents or interests in the same domain. The parents could be engineers or doctors and children could be talented and love music or painting.

Every person in any age wants to be popular, needs to be accepted and appreciated. Of course everybody is special although the person might not know why or where. The parents' job is to find what is so special about their child and then to help enrich the child's grow. Being special, exceptional in anything gives many benefits. One has the satisfaction, can by passionate about it. Others are noticing it and respecting. Someone who found any subject to be really good in it doesn't care that much about failure or trouble in other subjects.

The parents should remember how important is to notice, appreciate and to prize their children for smaller or bigger achievements. The prize should never have simple monetary value.

It is clear to everybody there are parents who can afford to pay for many kind of teachers, trainers for private lessons of any subject the children want. The other parents cannot afford for anything extra at all and they hardly provide food and shelter. Those who don't have money should find publicly available place where children can use and improve their knowledge and talents. Working on children's talent is usually learning something related to school program then students can use the public library assistance. Unfortunately in most domains achieving high level requires high financial spending. For those without financial means using fully what is available for free only can lead to above average skills level.

The parents should remember from the very first day of they child that life is not only learning in school, working, improving skills, performing professional job. The social side of the life is very important too. Ability to be accepted and better yet be liked and respected among friends and all peers. More or less usefull is ability to find own place and group and being able to cooperate with others. For that purpose is good to have any skills on much higher than average level.

The parents should raise their child the way the child would know own value and thanks that would not let be discriminated or demean in any way.

In America they brainwash less bright people about self esteem. Oprah, Tyra Banks and many other fake gurus are creating defective opinions. The say everybody should feel good about himself or helself and should not change to be liked by others. The truth is when we think that one of our's qualities is great but many other people don't think that then most likely this quality is not important or has very little value. Specially Oprah and Tyra Banks are crying there is too much pressure for young children to look good, wear good clothes and have expensive toys. Those two fake feminists state that all useless, lazy, without any skills, uneducated overweight females should feel good and be happy they are what they are. Yes, right. Would any of those women want to be with a man who has very low paid job, comes from a work, wears baggie pants and oversized t-shirt, drinks beer and is watching games on televsion all evenings?

We all like attractive people. When we meet someone new first we see how that person looks like. Our unconscious creates most of the opinion about the person. Much later we notice how the person is reacting with us. When we begin conversation and learn more details about each other our opinion could change a little bit but in most cases is already too late for that.

It would seam not important for the children how attractive they are but the children turn into adults. For adults sexual attraction is the most important regardless if we want and can or we don't want or can't have any sexual relation with the other person. This attraction starts from good look what means the children from the youngest age should strive for being in shape with good health, atlethic handsome look and friendliness with others.

Self esteem, good health and familiarity with school material at the end of the primary school is base for new start in high school.

High school.

Going to high school is a huge step causing many changes in the child's life.

Usually changing is good.

Coming to the new school almost everything has clean start without previous problems.

The grades given by the teachers depend much less on who the parents are and more on the skills and learned knowledge. The parents' position still counts a bit. The children with important parents can count on receiving rounded up grades. The other nobody's children are not discriminated much though. The biggest difference for the children depended on their parents is in the most extreme situations. For two children with the same skills deserving the same the teacher can favor the child with more important parent and give a priviledge to this child.

Of course lack of social skills, justified or not standing up against a teacher will cause big problems and the teacher will with all power demean and discriminate trouble causing student. This is the reason why learning social skills and general primary school material is important to avoid making big mistakes in the high school.

Speaking of learning what is in prescribed program it should be easier because there are some profiles in high school and a student has to some degree possibility to choose subject according to own interests. The school profile gives more attention hopefully to the subjects favored by the student. The subject giving the student most trouble would be treated with less importance.

The parents as well as the children should very carefully consider choosing the high school.

The student in new high school thanks to own work, attitude and social behavior has possibility to find the most suitable social and educational position in community.

It is very important for the student to be fully aware of what to expsect in the high school and how to be the best prepared for it. It is a fact in the high school will be a few the same collegues from the primary school but it is not that important because they will have to establish own new position as well.

From educational point of view the student should do whatever is possible to do well specially on the few first tests, assignments and exams.

In the inter-student relations the new student should never ever let be demeaned or discriminated by anybody nor ever demean or discriminate others. At the same time it is good to show and use after school interests and skills to get accepted on the most favorable position.

During all time in the high school the student needs to know that acquired knowledge will be necessary and will be used in the rest of the productive life. When student choses going to college or university the high school material will be the base and constantly used during the study. Even going to work straight from high school the level of familiarity with school material will decide about the future carrier.

The high school students are in special age when a plenty is going on. The whole physical process of going into adulthood is associated with emotional growing. In the high school are created friendships often turned into the romances. Every student should be open for new aspect of the very own life and know how to avoid any future life destroying troubles.

The school learning is important and the involvement in the other interests, subjects are very important too. The high participation should take place. Over all learning all kind of new sports, improving already acquired sporting skills and growing physical strength. Arthistic aspect cannot be forgotten and every student should find what kind of art is into and check where it would lead to. As sily as it could seam for many music, painting, sculpting, theater, dancing and other arts could give a lot of satisfaction. More different subjects the student tries the easier will be decide what direction to choose for the whole future life.

Colleges and universities

Beginning study in a college or university young person is stepping into the almost adult life. School grades depend almost only on the ability to present acquired knowledge. What kind, how reputable the college is and what grades the student receive decide in the most part about future social status, financial level and quality of life. Of course all connection or lack of them have big meaning in everybody's life. For example a fresh doctor with influencial parents in medicine will have much easier way of finding the practice. Part of the absolvents will work for they parents or associates. The largest population of absolvents is just on their own to the rest of their life.

Every person has interests and talents in one or the other direction. This should always be taken in consideration while choosing education and jobs. On the other hand everybody should remember the need for food and shelter and ability to provide for own future family. Even the most interesting subject to study and work line to do have to satisfy the minimum of financial needs.

During university study the most attention should be paid to the subject the most useful in the future professional work.

Additional very important thing in the college time is finding the life partner. I say so because during college years the young people are already adult but they don't have all real adult life duties. The students have plenty of time for social life and staying in similar circles there is a lot of chances to find that special one. When study is finished they have to go every day to work, they get on many duties and contacts with other similar singles is rapidly limited. In addition old friends get busy with their own life and social networking narrows. Time is ticking and searching for love and long term relationship is more difficult, needs more time, energy and deep thinking it over. During university years everybody spends time among similar free spirited peers and relationships are happening effortlessly.

After the graduation every graduate needs to find a job and go through the rest of the adult life.

Good luck!

The diseases.

Hypertension

There are not known as yet neither the reasons nor the mechanisms of hypertension.

Yes, the temporary hypertension shows up during strong and rapid diseases or after complicated child birth.

In described above cases when the main sickness subsides the blood pressure returns to the normal level. Another case is when a person under high stress level starts to eat much more and in the short time gains significant amount of weight. When the condition of higher blood pressure is noticed and the patient goes back to the normal weight the pressure often lowers too. In all other cases the hypertension could be cause by civilization disease by too high stress in daily activities, chemicals in the food we eat or in the air we breath. It could be cause by higher and higher levels of radiation from radars, telecommunication or cosmic radiation. As I said before nobody really knows.

In my observation I noticed some back pain caused by stretching, pulling muscles could put pressure on something and temporarily lower blod pressure. It could be just a shock and pain or something connected to the spine.

When doctor recognizes hypertension the patient has to take a medicine. Usually it starts from small dose of one medicine which is not exclusive for hypertension and the same medicine could be used in other cardiovascular problems. After while it is not enough and the doses are increased and sometimes the patient needs to take few medicines simsultaniously. Since we don't know neaither the reason not any cure for hypertension the medicines are indirectly doing damage to the patiens by deluting blood, making vains weaker, softer, slowing down the heart action and other things. The hypertension medicines have known and accepted side effects as odema, cough, etc. Maybe it is doing damage to the body but it is better to do some damage and keep patient alive than don't damage anything and let hypertension to destroy liver, heart, kidneys. Many of the hypertension medicines have such action that after short while the patient has to keep taking it to the end. It is not a big deal because the patient has to take this or the other medicine for the rest of the life anyway. There are clever, mean people who say they were taking hypertension medication and after exercising or whatever they don't do it anymore. It is terrible lie. Even they really stop taking the medicine for short period they will have to resume and continue it. The worse is someone else listening to them could stop taking own medicine or experiment with the dosage causing more and unnecessary problem to own health. Usually the doctors are prescribing small dose at first and then they increase it until the blood pressure drops down to acceptable level. Any experimentation with lowering dosage by the patient is high degree of stupidity and anybody encouraging it has evil mean. For the first and the most we know nobody can cure hypertension then there is no point to believe someone is cured. Secondly stupid experiment with lowering dosage is not giving results immediately. Patient can think everything is without any change for 2, 3 days and the blood pressure stays on good level. After couple more days or a week the pressure jumps up and down what the patient could think as a good sign. After 10 days to 2 weeks the blood pressure goes up and stays up. When the patient understands the experiment failed is too late and resuming the original doctor's prescribed dose is not enough anymore. Because the doses are in 5 mg then the patient has to take one more pill a day costing about $1 a day or more what makes about $400 a year.

At least one of the hypertension medicines Norvasc is absorbed by the body 45% to 230% better with a presence of the grapefruit juice. It means depend on a patient drinking grapefruit juice while poping up the pill the patient could take only 0.4 to 0.7 of the pill. As I said earlier the doses are 5mg, 10mg, and so on and it is difficult to measure 0.7 of the pill. Secondly the body reaction on the juice could be changing then hypertension has to be very strictly monitored. The danger is any not monitored, unnoticed differences in the juice quality, fraction of the pill would cause changes in hypertension levels. Rocking the pressure levels might cause more problems. The conclusion is this kind of experiment is very difficult to control. All doctors want to earn more and more money and avoid any trouble not to pay very special attention to one of the patients. The doctors are not interested in slightest way in prescribing smaller doses of any medicine and more often they have commission from prescribing more or higher doses. There is no doctor in the world who would care enough and want to go to the extent of using grapefruit juice to lover a medicine.

Statistics show the people in North America are consuming too much salt. There is plenty or excessive amount of salt in most meals. We remember well breakfast sausages In hotel restaurants so salty they are hard to swallow. I do not like most of the favorite North American food choices and I think I do not consume too much salt. Research and statistics say lowering intake of salt, alcohol and begin excercising when someone was not moving would lower hypertension by 5-8 points.

Let's consider what lowering hypertension by 5-7 points mean.

The blood pressure 120/80 or lower is good and normal. The blood pressure 135-139/85-89 is increased and treated as the first warning. Anything higher than that is hypertension.

A doctor detecting the blood pressure 127/87 will assume it is OK and could be caused by the stress from visiting the doctor. One time measured blood pressure does not mean anything. Looks like this higher blood pressure would be detected only for hypochondriacs who are searching for own imaginary sicknesses. In case of most people this stage is never detected by the doctors. Only in case of blood pressure 128/88 the patient cutting intake of alcohol, salt and starting vigorous excercising could delay the day of beginning to take hypertension medication. After some time these people will have growing blood pressure and will start taking medicines.

For people with blood pressure 140/92 to 180/120 lowering pressure by 5-7 points to 135/87 to 175/115 using medicine is unavoidable.

As we see it is just empty talk about not taking the hypertension medicines and trying all natural methods like excercising, decreasing intake of salt and increasing intake of garlic, onion, bananas.

Of course not eating excessive amount of salt, not overdosing alcohol and having physically active life style is always good for everybody.

Refux acid.

Too much acid above or below stomach is commonly called reflux acid. Like most legends it has nothing to do with too much acid produced in the stomach.

People eating hard to digest meals can cause the stomach to increase production of the acid to help dealing with the food. As long as acid stays in the stomach everything is OK. When from time to time there is plenty of acid and pressure inside the stomach grows the upper or lower valve cannot keep it in and acid is flowing up or down causing unpleasant effects. The presence of acid outside the stomach is going unnoticed until it does some damage and patient feels sore throat continous coughing. Sometimes the acidic gas makes throat sensitive and small wounds in the tissue where bacterias could grow. This type of symptoms we can see in the restaurants and bars when alcohol drinking, heavy meal eating patrons are coughing a bit. When symptoms go away the next day nobody remembers and never associate it with reflux acid. When stomach is quite often overfilled with plenty of acids needed to digest heavy meals the disease becomes chronic. It is really mechanical problem and valves are not closing completely. There is no cure for it. Sure if the problem was in short time and patient stops eating much and never heavy meals the valve could repare by iself. Unfortunately after long lasting problem there is no cure at all. The only thing what could be done is taking a medicine reducing production of acid before every meal. Some people try going on diet and eating light meals in small amounts. Both way seams to give expected results for a year or two but later having less acids in the stomach is causing not enough processed food going down from stomach and slowly but surely it creates additional problems. Lower pressure in the stomach and less acid stop giving previous symptoms but weak valves are still weak. Later the stomach by itself will be producing less what is not enough acid for food processing and underprocessed food will keep going farther in digestive system. From this point on the patien will never ever be able to handle regular size heavier meals.

There are magicians and fraudsters who know other, "better" methods not recommended by pharmaceutical companies. One of such fake medicines is apple cider vinegar consumed right before the meal. It is rubbish and lie. Action of this vinegar is similar to alcohol and works like a shot of vodka or glass of wine before the meal. When we drink something acidic our stomach senses it and delays production of own acids and digestion but the provided liquid begins working immediately instead of waiting for stomach to create own acid. Magicians recommend special acid hardly available on the market to make business on it and to argue about not following instruction in case the patient uses any other equally working acid. When people are not cured they may think the vinegar was not right or whatever and lier magician is not exposed for fraud. Another action of consumed alcohol is it's absorbed and transported in blood everywhere including patient's brains causing slight addiction and fake satisfaction. In such case all liquids suggested by fraudsters could cause more problems than give cure for.

The legends and superstitions.

The falks wisdom

Everything what is commonly said and believed as a true is not true at all.

Common legends are the wisdom of the nation.

Sure they are. The smart nation is inventing rubbish, lies, legends and calls it a wisdom. The stupid people believe it is true and they are brainwashed. The smart nation knows it is not the true at all and is acting differently than common wisdom advices gaining a lot.

"When the sun sets in red it will be rain the next day or freezing day or whatever else."

The elder people don't even remember since when the old people have rheumatism, migrene or other problems. Those problems have stronger symptoms when the atmospheric pressure is changing. They feel headache, muscle and joint pain. The older people with lack of technology were more connected to the nature and associated own pains with weather changes. When an elder said there will be rain tomorrow or any other weather changes the youner people asked how could he know about it. Nobody would dare to admit the knowledge is from pain in joints because everybody would laugh and the elder would lose respect and status of special wisdom. The elder looked up in the sky to see clouds, the sun, the moon or stars and made up an explanation. The more strange and colorful it was the more people listened. We people are animals living in groups then we do what others around us are doing. In the so called wisdom others repeated any rubbish the elder said adding own two cents.

> "When rain creates bubles on the water surface it will be rainy weather for long time."

This is an excellent lie aspecially the length of the "long time" can be manipulated to anybody's liking. Sometimes in few minutes long time is enough specially that bubles stop appearing. Of course the are no bubles since the rain stopped.

The air components as any gas components are dissolving in the liquid like water. The amount of dissolved gases depends mostly on the pressure, temperature and artificial influence of a mechanical mixing. In the natural environment there is almost no mixing unless it is Niagara Falls what creates another story. When gas is leaving water sometimes the surface tension is keeping water around small gas quantities creating bubles. The surface tension is what it is and it not depends on how long the rain will be lasting. The surface tension could be stronger when water contains pollutant chemicals. When we add soap to water in a bathtub we have a buble bath. In the nature water contamination stays constant unless very dirty rain is falling creating increased amount of bubles. When drops of rain water are heating the water surface the energy of collision is kicking small amount of gas out of water what helps creating bubles. The more gas want to leave water the more bubles show up. It is associated with degree of saturation. When maximal saturation level is decreasing then more gas has to leave water. The maximal saturation depends on temperature and pressure. When athmospheric pressure is dropping down than water can hold less and less gas and gas is leaving creating bubles.

Conclusion one is the bubles are created when front of law athmospheric pressure is rapidly coming in.

We can notice that not whole surface of the observed water is the same. Where water is shallow and without currents (is not mixing) the water temperature is higher. When temperature is higher more gas exceeds saturation level and has to leave. Rain drops are kicking more bubles on shallow warmer part of the water surface. In addition when rain is warm than the rain is warming up whole water, mixing it and crates more bubles.

The conclusion is the most bubles are created on static, shallow water during fall of warm rain, specially when low athmospheric front is rapidly coming.

"Example from Urulu – Ayers Rock in Australia."

Millions of years ago rapid athmospheric conditions like tempists, rains, cyclons as well as geological events like eruptions of volcanos created cooled down Earth crest. During the next millions years the crest was broken into the main pieces. Over 20 milions years ago movements of tectonic plates broke a piece of it and pushed one end down inside the Earth. The other end of this piece of plate was sticking up. For the next millions years the erosion of rock mixed with water was creating dirt and dust and soil covering everything. Later falling rains were cleaning sticking up top of the tectonic plate. This piece of the rock is sticking a little bit up above the earth surface and most of it is deep down under the ground. When we see this top only it it looks like someone put there a really big smooth rock on the ground.

The elders living in this part of Australia tell stories about this rock creation. They say there were two giant brothers bored to death who took mud and created irregular ball. They put this piece of mud on the ground, looked at it and said "We created something good."

I believe that comparing the mud ball with millions year natural tectonic creation of Ayers Rock is stretched beyond the absurd.

A Hawaiian legends tell a god took out a rock from the ocean water and created this or the other island. Of course when something is sticking out of the water most people don't try to persuade anybody that this island dropped down from the sky. On the other hand it is true that when rocks from the bottom of the ocean are reaching above the water surface they are called islands. It is not important if the lowered level of ocean surface uncovered something what was under water or tectonic movements pushed piece of rock up or volvcanic lava was collecting until it created the island.

All people always want to have respect, fame and to be known as wise. The smarter cheaters are making up stories colorizing it and are telling it in the most interesting way. The others are listening and appreciating so called wisdom.

On a slippery road up hill or in deeper snow the car's wheels are losing traction and is difficult to drive. When a driver is not sure what to do then so called bad meaning wizards are telling the driver not to press accelerator. It is an excellent adviece because when the drive cannot manage everybody can laugh and demean the driver. Later one of the so called wizards gets in the car presses gas pedal to the metal and makes to the top of the hill. It is the truth that driving on slippery road up hiil or not we should never rapidly press or rapidly release excelerator pedal becase wheels would lose the traction. As I said the car would lose the traction. Going up hill on slippery road the car is just losing most of the traction already and wheels are begining turning loose. To gain a bit more traction and make to the top we need to accelerate more and if needed to the max. When the wheels are losing traction the car is going uncontrollable backward down. There is still some small traction and running wheels faster and faster we get more of this fractional tracton until we gain enough to pull car up and the car inertia can help a bit too. We have to add excelleration fast but not too rapidly and with some luck we succeed. Adding little or no gas we lose more and more traction until gravity is stronger and we fail. Worse come to worst and slow acceleration while hardly moving is making the surface more slippery in one place.

We need to add enough gas before the surface under the wheels turns more slippery and use partly car inertia partly traction to drive to the top of the hill.

"The nice calf can suck two cows."

Absolutely not! There was a song about two horses. One was mean and dangerous another nice obeying the carter. The mean horse had some gains and the nice one was only bitten. When someone is nice and obeys orders nobody pays attention to the needs of the person he meets mostly ignorance. The preson is used and abused by anybody. The carter was afraid of the mean horse then fed it well and never put too heavy load on the carrage. To suck two cows the person has to be without honor, ambition. When they kick him out, spit on him he says it was just a rain and is coming through another door to kiss asses until he gets what he wants.

"The house is a great investment."

It is true when the parents buy a house for $200,000, pay about $450,000 for the mortgage, they add another $100,000 for improvements and maintenance. After many years the children inherit the house and sell it for $300,000. Sure it is great investment the children never spent a penny but for parent's $200,000 house they've got $300,000.

The cats are sitting above underground water ducts. Yes, right. The cats seat where they can watch without being seen and where they can have two ways for running out. They seat where they get used to. They seat where people do because it must be good place since the "big cat" is seating there so often.

We can summarize the people are repeating other peoples stories, legends when they have nothing to say on they own. Most of the time they don't know if there is any truth in the story. Few others know it is not truth but they reapeat it hoping someone would believe and make mistakes. The knowledge is valuable.

"Opinion about how to solve a problem."

Those who say it is easy usually have no clue what it is all about then it is easy for them to say anything. Very few people know the problem very well and could say it is not difficult to solve it. For all others every new problem has some degree of difficulty.

"Democracy in Greece."

We are told the first democracy was created in Greece. After careful consideration we see the whole system was created in such way that it was easy to discriminate, destroy or ban anyone from the town. The smartness in this democracy was that everyone had one vote but it is always easy to manipulate most voters and later wash out hands from the consequences.

We hear there is a free press and they publish articles about someone's wrong doing. There are writings full of numbers, information pretending the media inform public about something and let to gain knowledge. There is a special science how to write in a newspaper. Given numbers have to be set the way nobody could know anything more after reading it. The simpliest way to do it is to describe part of the subject (like how much part of the considered group costs or earns or owns or gains...) in dollar value. The second part is given as a fraction of the whole. The third part is described in percentage increase from the value in previously reported time in the past. The fourth part is given as a dollar value in difference to the fifth part. The rest is left undescribed. All data, numbers could be true but just in case the described whole is divided to non exclusive parts with complicated common elements. It is done this way to make sure that even the most pedantic, curious reader cannot compare newspaper data with reality and calculating, recalculating, comparing will never ever give anything useful to be gain from the reading. One more very important role is the editor has to keep track of it to make sure the same facts are always given in the same way because otherwise some stubborn readers could wait a couple of years, compile couple of writings and get a piece of true information from it. The second easy way of misleading is purposely making an error. They switch two digits in one number or say decrease instead of increase. Most readers read it and gets fouled by it. When someone more important demands to clear erroneous information then a few weeks later in very small print unnoticed by anybody apologies are written still not giving out what the mistake was. Reporters are using and abusing human mistakes as well. When gasoline price went up 20 cents per litre a reporter was talking to gas station customers complaining about the cost of gas. The reporter asked how much more people have to pay now wih compare to yesterday. One person said full tank 60 litres by 20 cents is $1.20. The man didn't calculate correctly because 60 litres by 20 cents is $12. He would get really angry if he could count.

The reporter never pointed out the mistake and the media air out only mistaken opinion to brainwash the whole population.

Let the more stupid person win because he is more stupid anyway. Rubbish! Only the more stupid lets undeserved win to the smarter one because he is more stupid as we said. The smarter one never let go and manipulates the others until he sets thing as desired. It doesn't matter that jokingly he admits being stupid because at the end he wins anyway. Manipulating all the time and being happy with own skills is not too smart because sooner or later others are pushed away.

We use term intelligence in describing people but nobody thinks what it means. It has nothing to do with person's wealth, position, education. The intelligence is an ability to manipulate others for own benefits. That's why they call terrorists, spies who are killing, bribing and spreading falsified information, turn down governments in other countries as the intelligence.

Many say the saving is the best way to achieve financial goals. What a lie! Nobody ever became richer by saving. One can get richer by earning more. When someone would go bankrupt in 5 years and the one is saving like crazy the person can go bankrupt in 6 years. Right, but he already lives for all the 6 years like a bankrupt or worse. Sure you can turn poor when you waste money for example after the paycheck the person is drinking alcohol, buying drinks for others and later has no money for food. One can get poor rapidly buying gifts for easier going women. There is no good enough gift for any woman and she expects more and more the next time.

I know a real example of young couple who decided to save money by living for 5 years with parents instead of renting any own place. The saved money suppose to build nice down payment for their new house. They did as they said. While living together the tension between them and the parents was growing until they could not stand it anymore, they were close to divorce and 4 years later had to move out. They didn't collect enough money then they had to take mortgage for the new house on very difficult terms. They don't have any relation with their parents ever since. The younger brother never cared about money he was buying nice cars, clothes and taking his fiancé on expensive vacation. When he's got married there was no consideration to live with parents. He didn't have a penny for downpayment then the parents gave him the whole downpayment. He is still the most favorite son in the world.

Prodigal children

There is an opinion the parents collected a great wealth and the son wasted it all.

It could be truth sometimes when a father treated badly his son, never respected him, never thinks about the son as equal to him and always have too high expectations. The son could get rebellious and do everything possible against and in spite of the father.

There are few different cases in wasting family wealth. The first case is when the wealth was dishonestly gathered. Let's say the Bill Gates passes all his wealth to the honest son. In 5 years the most of the Microsoft would not exist. There are many small businesses exsisting only because the owner is cheating on customers and taxes. The honest son doing the same business honestly adhering to the law may couse the business to cease existence. Just the ownership change from the father to the son can catch someones attention and after extended audit the business is bankrupt or taken by the government.

The next case is when the father had many connections and relations with cooperators and customers. When the son gets management and is getting into the connection to fast he could make a wrong move and old connections stop working and business goes down. Sometimes the father is doing very well but times are changing and business has to be flexible accommodating new times. When the father cannot catch up with all the changes the business is going slower and slower although from the outide everything seams to be OK. The collected capital is used on daily operations. Very often there is so much stress the father gets sick or dies. The son taking over the business can do very little to keep it and he loses it all. Outsiders think it is the son's fault but really the father would lose it too.

The very specific case is when the father makes more of his fortune during the war and his son who lives in peacefull time cannot keep the same business. Usually the wars were every other generation.

One of the most likely cases is when the father found a niche and made a fortune in one domain. The son could have talents in something else. The son could be an artist or scientist. If the son don't have a nose in the same thing what the father has than the son cannot expand the father's business. The people don't realize that if you don't improve, expand your business you are losing it all. I think about 1/3 is often lost because of unexpected political, economical, life changes. It could be because changes in political, international system, wars, restrictions or the stock exchanges correction. The earthquakes, floods, hurricanes could cause loses too. Any plags of insects, pandemia can cause all enterprises involving plants, animals are going down. The true or made up cow diseases cause blocking export of meat. The rest of 2/3 of the business value the owner has to hide somewhere and fight for it all the time to prevent other businesses or government taking over. If there is anyone well connected who wants take over someone's business he can send a taxman. The taxmen incestigation not only interrupts normal business activities by taking over documents and employees time but can easily cause banking problems for the firm. Greedy dishonest people and government try to take as much as possible regardless what law says. When the business owner doesn't know how to properly fight with them at least half of everything could be taken away. When people know about someone's wealth they try to sue the person for everything what is possible and impossible. The more money one has the more people know about it and more and stronger they want to take it. It is much easier to take from someone else than work and earn by yourself. Summarizing when 1/3 is lost by unexpected situation or accident. From the rest 1/3 is taken illegally by others or by the government then the owner is left with just 1/3 of his business. It could be not enough for the son to keep conducting the business and live on the same level as his father.

The people with the nose for the business.

I've always wondered what is with this nose for the business.

There are stories, legends, movies about children, mostly sons of very rich people who go to Europe for couple of years and after the return they are great leaders in the business.

It is really like in the following description. The sons of very rich fathers were going to Italy or other European countries under a pretext to study. They didn't do much else than drinking, partying, taking drugs, using prostitutes or seducing women. Sooner than later they were in collision with the law. For one they could make women pregnant or involve in car accident while drunk or damage to property or bar fighting. They spend there so much money and made so many debts that even for their well established parents it is difficult to clean it up. At this point the father had to send own security guard to clean debts, take care of criminal charges and bring prodigal son back home. It is impossible for such spoiled, recless, very often addicted to drugs and alcohol young ignorant to change into reputable business man. What was happening is the father began taking his son with him and introduced the son to all business partners, cooperators and customers as the future heir. The father was keep doing business as usual and the son has plenty of time to understand all connections. One would think that such son couldn't be better than other people finishing higly reputable universities. Actually finishing university and having knowledge of work in the business makes doing business very difficult.

An example.

Would anybody with knowledge and common sense want to do business with solar panels generating electiricity? Of course not! It is financially impossible. The business people on the other hand can make money on it. How it is done was described much earlier in this book. Time is passing by and smartness and fraudulency is growing. It could be someone dare to audit solar panels generation station. The busness owner says they cannot produce enough electricity because there is too much CO_2 in Earth athmosphere. They've got another "brilliant" idea. They want to throw away solar panels and make more money on it. How? It's simple. They want to send those panels to the Moon or in Space. Now they could get so much taxpayers money from the government. Nobody cares that government is grabbing taxes from hard working people who hardly have enough for food and shelter. The businessmen can take as much money as they want for producing solar panels. They don't have to produce anything because the public will not see those panels in the Space anyway.

This is the way of doing business for all large corporations. They associate themselves with similar others. They create inconceivable lies to brainwash general population and all benefits, income is coming from the taxes only.

Let's take another example. When in a firm the costs are too high they need to cut employees. Who can do it better? Those knowing real business educated people or greedy, reckless one?

Anyone who knows would check who is doing what and let go to those who are useless and earning a lot of money. In result there would be plenty of savings but those cusins, associates, cooperators and their associates would not be paid at all. All specialists would stay at work. The best specialists will not save the firm because profit is not related to the product quality at all. In addition all those fired associates will cut all connections and stop allowing dealing and wheeling behind the scenes and the firm cannot continue activity.

The ruthless consultant will check who has connections and fires all others making more than average money. In this scenario less money is saved on cut salaries and skilled workers are out the door. All well connected without whistle blowers will redirect the firm in another more profitable line of work.

To have a nose for the business.

There are people listening around to find who has the power and who makes large scale businesses. Thsese with so called nose people do anything possible to suck to the powerfull ar at least try to imitate the powerfull people action on very small scale.

The experts

Who are the experts?

It sounds so serious.

The experts are the people who finished two, three weeks experts training course. During their training they learn appropriate attitude.

The experts act very sure of themselves. They never hesitate before they give the answers.

The experts are using very strong words like "yes", "no", "always", "never", "you have to", "you mustn't" etc. They tell what others have to do or have to not do and what terrible will happen when someone doesn't follow the advice.

The statistics show the expert's predictions are wrong in 80% of the cases.

The experts have very limited knowledge about the subject of their expertise. It is a good thing because they don't have to understand what they are saying and without any deeper knowledge they never hesitate with the answers.

Why anybody needs the experts or is listening to the experts?

It is simple. In a business world the business owners have to make decisions and they have to live with the consequences. They never need any experts.

In the business there are plenty of people who are not the business owners but they make decisions. The good decisions bring profits and prize from the business owners. The bad decisions bring loses, sometimes terrible loses and deserve punishments. To avoid being punished by business owners the decision makers use the experts to cover their behinds. The more experts and the more serious sounding experts supported the bad decision the better is the excuse. How could you punish for the bad decision if there were so many experts supporting it?

Just listen for once what the experts say and you'll know how shallow their knowledge is. Not to mention any experts who are paid to give the wrong advices.

About human intelligence.

The children are born with talents in this or that and with lack of talents in something else. Everything depends on how they are directed in the beginning part of their life. When the parents notice child's special talents in anything they can send the child to classes, trainings making this talent thriving. When the talents in the early childhood goes unnoticed it can be totally wasted forever. The other aspect in education of young children is almost any child encouraged, a bit forced, persuaded, pushed by any tricks can gain above average skills in something. The parents need to be smart and learn if the child has special talent in this domain or does it only because is forced to do so. In any case the learning process has to be well balanced to not deprive the child of normal life appropriate for the child's age. When children don't have normal childhood than even they become world champions, famous all over the world later they very often are unfit to live normal life.

Regardless of any special talents every person needs skills to communicate with others, cooperate with others and to find acceptance in social life.

Sometimes problem is caused by raising children in military like system. In such system there are rewards and punishments. The rewards are very rare because the reward should be for special achievement only and opportunities for such achievement are rare. The rewards could be expensive making them more rare. There is no reason for punishment unless the child does something very wrong. In this case the parents are left with possibility to allow or disallow something only. In such military style system any child understands very soon that parent can only forbid or allow something. The child knows that asking, begging, negotiating, doing voluntary chores will not change (unlike in the real world) the parents decision and any action could be turn against the child wishes. The children know the forbidding is the only control the parents have over them. Those children never ask for anything because this could give the parents opportunity to say no specially because it gives away what is important for the child at this moment. These children are growing without necessary skills for asking, negotiation, bargening and are not well fit for life. To get what they want the children are pretending they don't care or are asking for something opposite hoping the parents wanting to show the control would do opposite to expressed by child request and actually give them what they really wanted in the first place.

When soldier expected guests visiting his home asked his commander for not giving him additional duty for the next day. The commander gave him additional duty just to prove who's the boss. The next time when the same soldier expected guests went to the commander and asked for additional duty because his wife wanted to do general cleaning at home. After a while the commander told the soldier he cannot assign any duties for him. The soldier has got what he really wanted.

The skills and talents are not related in any way to the intelligence. Please notice there is IQ score in America but it has notihing to do with intelligence either. As researches show people with higher IQ are not getting better carrier and don't have better achievements than those with lower IQ. Of course, lower and higher IQ in certain range. I'm not comparing two people with IQs 150 and 30. The IQ score is false because two different people answering the same number questions correctly could get different IQ score. What kind of testing system it is since anybody could get prepare (get familiar with type of questions and variants of questions and answers) in 2,3 weeks for the test and score significantly higher. The IQ test is just rubbish. We well know there are no three easy lessons of smart thinking.

Inteligence is the ability to manipulate others.

In common meaning lying is something wrong. Evrrybody lies anyway. The animals lie too. Of course if we define lie as telling something what is not true the animal don't talk. How do we call cameleon behavior of pretending is blended in the background? What about wild animals waiting for a pray when they do not move and pretend they sleep or don't see until the pray comes close enough for sure catch? What about quail pretending injury and difficulty in movements just to lead someone away from the nest and when they are far away the quail takes off in the air and disappears? The lie and intelligence are very close and very connected to each other. There are no lies in politics but only any possible action to achieve goal. The action like signing peace treaty or pretending the attack was mistaken just to gain time to regroup, better arm and attack on unexpected again.

The men's chcracter flaw are very often described and often ridiculed by comediants. To keep book title spirit I'll write more about women.

The women are more intelligent than men are. I mean it. The man needs facts and analysis to make decision what take long sometimes too long time. The woman makes emotional and in the most cases right decision immediately.

All girlfriends, granmothers, mothers, aunts, older cousins are teaching the young women how to use sex to manipulate men. In common saying the man should never manipulate women. Why is it that only men who can manipulate women are popular and women are flocking around them? Anybody heard women ever said the men who manipulates women is bad and they avoid him? No, the women are running after those manipulators. On the other side when a man doesn't let to be manipulated by woman and tells her that honestly he is portrayed by her and others as the worse kind in the world.

The women act in erratic way changing plans, opinions and expectations all the time. When man loves a woman he let her keep doing it and after short while the woman calls him whimp and leaves him. This behavior has the only purpose to find a man who doesn't let her jerk around. When she sees he is stronger and keeps control the woman knows he is the one and she relaxes. The women almost never lie because in their way of thinking lie doesn't exist. There is only being agreeable, sweet and nice when they want the man and keep fighting, complaining and doing everything to defy the man when they don't want to have sex with. The fraction of the men knows how to manipulate women. At the beginning they pretend they listen, they memorize one or two details and use it to show how much they suppose to care but it ends the minute they get the woman in bed.

The women manipulate men saying they were used for sex. Didn't women have pleasure too? Is sex no pleasure for women? Using for sex really means to brainwash or scare the woman to have sex with others and deny her all payments or other benefits.

The most and the most often people (men as well as women) lie in the business. I'm not going to get deep in it. Just one example. Someone high in the hierarchy tells workers there is demand for products and for short period of time workers should work overtime. After few weeks on Thursday the best before any long weekend there is a party with cake to celebrate the success. The very next day on Friday the workers get paycheck and pink slips. They are no longer needed.

When Bill Gates and Warren Buffett met students in a university in Nebrasca they were asked what skills, qualities are necessary to advance carrier in a corporation. Both agreeable never mentioned neither any skills for performing any profession nor an education. They said the most important is ability to manipulate others. The preffered is to be able recognize what skills has each employee or what skills they lack, gather those employees in a useful groups and then assimilate to the group. The second needed ability is to persuade others and use them the most at work. The people who have both of above described abilities and can manipulate anybody and everybody will advance the fastest.

The people who could learn many skills, performing different tasks could also learn how to manipulate others. Everything depends how they were raised at home. When children are tought honesty, importance to learn high skills to perform any specific tasks they have future closed and they will never advance their carrier. No manager will ever promote them to higher position. Why would he? The person is very good and usefull at the current position. The managers are not idiots and they don't want to lose a very useful employee. In the other homes the children think they are the center of the universe and everybody should serve them and prize them like it was shown in the movie about Kennedy family. These children learn manipulation from the youngest years and they know it is easier to manipulate someone else to do a job than do the job themselve. This kind of childhood creates the most successful people in the business.

Many people have ability to manipulate others. Manipulating has to be smart to give benefits and not alienate others. Otherwise it is turning against the manipulator. When as children or later people notice that they attractive look and interpersonal skills give them more or better results than other then those people manipulate more oftem and they are honing their skill. Too much even a dog can't eat. The smart people manipulate in important situations and just for sport or training sometimes only. They observe others reaction. Nobody likes to be manipulated and we don't like people who manipulate us too often. There are people who think they can make anybody to do whatever they want them to do. This is not smart at all because manipulating someone one time too many you lose everything. In such cases manipulation goes well for some time but manipulated people start feeling bad and slowly or rapidly they cut the influence and any relation with manipulator. When manipulated person is too weak to cut it off the person obeys for little longer and then does something against the manipulator. At work used employee is good and does not cause any trouble but when the line is crossed they do something dramatic on they own or in the worse moment they turn against the manipulator. As I said the smart people use manipulation only when it is really worth and when it causes to lose friends they don't care because it was worth it.

I don't say the women are worse than men. In fact very often the women are better than men. I'm just saying the women are different than men. They act, react and communicate differently.

The women are proud of their manipulation skills and often become the victims of they own actions. When a man says something then the words have meaning close to their description in a dictionary. When woman talks her words have very little meaning. Imprtant is her behavior and unverbal message. When BFF are in a store with clothes one never tells her friend this clothes don't suit her. The girlfriends are excited about every piece in the store but only unverbal reaction let one guess what the other thinks. In a group with women only they all can talk at the same time and men wonder who is listening. Nobody needs to listen because information is passed nonverbally. While training fiancé or future husband a woman says she does not want something but nonverbally she gives him a signal she wants it. Honest, stupid simple men do as they are told to do and they are scolded for it or sent to a dog house. Average smart men do opposite what women tell them to do and at the beginning of relation they are appreciated. It doesn't work later in time because women ar not that simple minded. Men in love let their love objects for all kind of manipulation. Sooner or later even the most stupid most in love man understands that woman of his dreams is manipulating him and what she says has nothing to do with what he should really do or what is expected from him. After years of beying together every man has enough of manipulation and becomes indifferent and uninterested. He just wants to have peace in mind and is not listening to anything what his woman says. At this point women are lamenting about husband's lack of emotion and that husbands don't want to please their wifes anymore. They've got what they wanted after years of teaching that words have no meaning.

In enterprising and in politics manipulation employees, coworkers, enemies and friends is necessary to such degree the lying, defrauding inferior subordinates is done on daily basis. One has to be careful to not make mob angry because it could lead to unexpected and undesired avalanche of reactions.

Poor elders with millions.

From time to time there is a gossip going that there was an old woman living like on very limited income but after her death turned out she had great wealth. After close look we see she left a house, a car, $100,000 in a bank and insurance policy. Total value is about half a million. It sounds a lot for a person living so quietly. Let's count it again. The car has value $300 then it is not worth to be mention. The house, as for the most older people, is free of mortgage of course. How could they afford any payments? They whould have to sell it and move out. $100,000 in a bank is not little but she was alone with nobody to count on and she needed money in case of sickness or disability. She was saving money living like animal in a shelter. Insurance policy for $30,000 only just to cover her funeral. The house value seams to be high about $400,000. Let's count it again The car is worthless, the house $400,000 in a bank $100,000 and insurance $30,000. The total is $530,000 what is still a lot. How much it really is? The insurance will cover the funeral. Selling the house costs about $30,000 and without the owner the house will go very low. From the money in bank need to be paid all kind of taxes. In real life all of it would give about $350,000 what is not very little. How much this woman was worth alive? About $90,000 from the bank minus taxes. She had to live in the house. Additionaly she had to pay for utilities and taxes. Most of the normal old people are worth more death than alive. At the end of the life the people hardly meet ends and when they pas away their value is suddenly higher.

How to understand simple things.

From the younger years I couldn't understand few simple things.

- How to dry a surface using wet rag.

    As long as there is plenty of water we can wet the rag and squeeze the water to the bucket. We keep drying this way. At one point there is little of water just about as much as stay in the rag after sqeezing. The rest of the water will always stay undried on the surface.

- When you don't know how to spell a word or how to do something check in a dictionary or ask.

    You don't know that you don't know. We think we know but we could be mistaken. When we doubt we can ask or check in the dictionary and we should. Nobody can check every word or always ask about everything. The teacher should correct all errors and explain how it all should be done. Later the teacher should ask the student to do it again and again until it is all done correctly.

- Don't bully the weaker. If you are so smart then bully someone stronger than you.

    As the name says the stronger is stronger and it is impossible to overpower someone stronger. When we can overpower someone stronger we become the stronger and we bully the weaker ones. The world is bad and the stronger always abuse the weaker ones.

- How a man could take advantage of a woman.

In what way a man can take advantage of the woman? Ok, he befriended her, she trusted him, he's got info about her and took her identity and her valuables. Yes, but it is not taking advantage but pure fraud, criminal activity. They say he used her for sex. How did he do it? Did they have sex and he didn't pay for the service? It is not taking advantage of the woman but dishonest business transation. How else he could use her? Maybe he sent her to have sex with other men and he didn't share the payment? This is pimping and prostitution. How else he could use her? Was he coming to visit her only when he wanted to have sex and later didn't call or didn't see her for a long time until the next visit? Yes, and she didn't have any pleasure during sex? They were using each other for sex. If she didn't have any pleasure why did she do it? Maybe she is so terrible that nobody tolerates her presence. Maybe she was paying with sex for his company?

Men's menopause.

Let's start with women. The girls in North America promise themself to lose virginity during the prom night at the latest. When the girl does not have a boyfriend there is a chance she would go to bed with someone who will be around at that time. A few girls get pregnant at the prom night. Many of them get married and live as family for many years. They both take care of food, shelter and they provide for the family in the best way they can. They raise their children together. When such a girl becomes a fourtysomething years old woman she is most likely financially independent. Their children are on their own already. When the woman think about her life with a man she was never crazy in love with she feels disappointed. She thinks she could find someone else for passionate sex, someone to fall in love with and she could experience everything what she missed in her life. Can we say she's got crazy or menopausal? Of course, not. There is nothing wrong with wanting passionate love or having sex with younger very attractive men specially that she's never done it before.

Let's go back to the men's menopause. Everybody, man or woman could have permanent or temporary sexual problems, regardless of the age. With years our body becomes weaker and physical effectiveness is going down. The men's menopause was just invented by the women to make them feel better hoping that physical and sexual changes are not exclusive for the women only. They say the men crossing fourty years age are experiencing the menopause because they check out young girls. Rubbish! There always were and always will be the most attractive women age from 16 to 23. The 16 years old for those very fast maturing only. There are women 30 years old who look much better than when they were 22 years old but it means they were immature emotionally for too long. Those women most likely physicaly would look better at the age 22 but they didn't care for presenting themselve well. When a boy had sex at the prom and girl got pregnant he married her. He was taking care of her, the children. To do it he was working hard very often overtime and had no free time for anything. Maybe he married the woman he was madly in love with and still had no free time for anything and didn't see the world except his wife. He is a man over fourty now. The children are on their own. He paid of the mortgage and since he is keep earning the same amount suddenly he has more money to spend. This guy can slow down hard work and look around. He will of course notice passing by young 16 to 23 years old women and as usual they look the best at this age. This man will not check out 60 years old women. Every boy and most girls wanted to drive a sport convertible car. Our guy couldn't ever afford to buy one and had to drive old Chevy instead. Being at fourty, for the first time debt free with spare money he will buy the dream of his life the sport convertible car. Driving with open roof he will check out passing by young then prietiest women. In case he is divorced and once have opportunity to have sex with young woman why would he say no? Is it men's menopause?

In the other case a guy could make pregnant a girl he was not madly in love with. They lived together for many years providing for the family and paying debts. In the middle age they both are financially independent without any obligations. Is it wrong he doesn't want to spend the rest of his life lovelessly and both want devorce and chance to find great passionate love? After divorce he has opportunity to meet and have fun with young women what he really missed earlier in his live. What's wrong in it? Only if he wants to marry very young girl or have a relation with much younger woman than something could be wrong with him. It is completely different story to have sex with much younger woman than to find spiritual connection and equity. It is happening when the young girl is very passive, with low selfesteem and the older guy tricks her into a relation. This guy is treating her like a toy, pays for what she wants and never expects anything else except sex. In extreme situation the older guy might be an inept who can't communicate with women in his age and is able to be a partner with very young inexperienced or already hurt by other men girl.

How is it a menopause? Which of the cases described above could fit such term?

Be yourself

To be yourself? It is the most idiotic idea destroying the whole future.

To have own style? O, yes! It is a good thing.

What is a style? How to have own style?

You have to find something commonly accepted but rearly seen. We have to like it and it has to fit us. We are going to use it to be a bit different than others.

We need to remember the life and the world is keep changing. The fashion and what is accepted is changing too. We cannot stick strictly to the chosen thing called style. We have to keep changing it too and adopting to the taste of others. Do you see it? "The taste of others". How is it our style then?

For example when a girl picked black dress to wear she is different than others and is wearing black color. This could be her style. When mini is in fashion she wears black or mostly black mini dress or black mini skirt. When leather is in fashin she picks black leather pants, skirts or dresses. When jeans are in fashon she picks dark jeans in very modern shape with few black accessories. And so on and on. You cannot always wear very similar kind of outfit because in short time it is changing from stayle to quirk.

For example actress Diane Keaton showed up wearing strange outfit and everybody said she has a style. She is wearing similar things after many years and nobody likes it. She is out of style. It is very similar in any life's domain like music, painting, architecture, film.

To be yourself is very bad idea. Explaining that one has to be himself is very shallow and full of it. It is just touching one aspect which actually excludes being ourselves.

Let's consider who is the person the each of us.

Human body does not like to get tired because it uses valuable components absorbed from the consumed food.

In this aspect nobody likes to work because work makes us tired. It is truth some people like what they do. I did like my professional work too but what we like it is only a fraction of whole aspect of working.

The artists can be themselve because it gives them individuality and very specific style.

Have you known any musicians playing in bands? Where they always talking how they don't like those gigs they are performing and would preffer to play something else. Let's take example of the Guitar Shaman Carlos Santana. He composed and played many pieces of music and people all over the world loved it. When he went for the first time to a disco in London he was surprised they play one of his songs. After a while he began to compose and play what he liked the most and what a muse was bringing him without considering taste of audience. In result he disappeared form the world's music scene for very long time.

Do you like singing in the shower? To be yourself sing it to the public. Why you don't do it? Because, they would laugh at you.

You are a pretty girl. When you put on underwear you dance in front of the mirror. If you are yourself dance the same way in a disco. You would never do it, right? Professionals lie to us and say dancing is an improvisation, demonstrating own feelings then why never ever anybody sensitive, expresionate became the best ballet dancer in the world over the night? Everybody who wants to achieve anything in dancing has to train, practice and repeat invented by choreographer the same movements all over and over again many hours every day for many years. Later they look straight into our eyes and talk how natural they are.

You are a good employee, you know your job and you do it very well. Your boss tells you to do something useless or badly designed. Be yourself and tell your boss that this task is poorly design, useless or unsafe. You don't because you musn't be yourself. The only think you could do is mention to your boss something valuable and make it look like it was bosses idea. Only then there is a chance you are told to do what you wanted in the first place although your boss should know it and make requests coming from his knowledge.

You are a woman and you are well aware the makeup, hair dye is bad for you hair and your skin but you are using it anyway. Why aren't you yourself and go out without makeup, powders, hair gel, pushup bra? Why do you cover most likely imaginary flaw in your beauty? Why you are not yourself? Because nobody would like you, nobody would want you.

You are honest person and you don't like lies. How come social studies show that in the first 10 minuts when friends meet each of them lies at least 3 times? Very often you know when your friend lies to you then why you don't point out those lies?

You are pretty woman and you like cookies and chocolate very much. Why don't you eat plenty of chocolate, cookies but you carefully watch what you eat and do anything you can to stay skinny?

You were stopped by a traffic officer who set a trap by planting poorly visible too low speed limit in unnecessary place. He was hiding the police car. You well know the police do it all to generate revenue and they don't care about road safety at all. Why you are not yourself and don't tell the officer to fight crime instead setting traps on honest taxpaying people? Do it and he will taser you till death or he'll bit you until you lose conscious.

Just a thought

There is a lot of talk about Holy Grail. What is it? Does it exist? For ages the symbol for medicine, doctors and anything related to health is a goblet with two intertwined snakes. Sometimes we think it is good and bad interconnected with each other.

Following other people ideas I though the snakes could symbolize DNA and the goblet could be a device used to modify DNA. Maybe the ancient civilizations or the aliens from outer space could do genetic modifications and the knowledge was passed to new generations or is hidden somewhere to prevent unefficient scientists from doing damage to all living creations.

Maybe, but I doubt it is the way to eliminate from human DNA all health problems, abnormalities. Later from generation to generation eliminating everything what is bad people would create the perfect human race. Some dream that in the future when we need wings we could genetically add wings to the next generation, when we need fins we could add fins too.

This is most likely utopia because eliminating one thing another problem would be created. The newer generations would always need more and something new and there always would be samething bad.

If this is the Holy Grail it is better it is hidden and mean men cannot create monsters or terrible diseases. Unefficient scientists would create new race with terminal handicaps or maybe our mortality is one of these DNA modification results.

There is possibility the Evil Alien or any Deamon from Space began genetic modifications on humans what led to denaturalization, deseases and bad meanings.

It is possible the ancient civilization performed genetic modification and in result almost all humans died except few untouched by civilization and the experiment who survived and continue recovery all human race from beginning.

Is bad meaning coded in human genes?

I was thinking why people do so mach evil to everybody and everything around. Is bad meaning in our genes?

If it is in the genes than is it as result from an experiment going wrong or maybe we need it to survive.

It looks like all bad human qualities like need for superiority, excessive greed, deriving pleasure from harming others, overwhelming sexual desires are very useful and necessary to survive.

Yes, it causes many disasters, unjustice, wars, morders, abuse, and so on. Without those qualities there would not be advances neither in science and technology nor much intellectual development.

If people would not act mean just for fun and would not want more than they need we would be still seating under the fruit tree. From time to time someone would get up to pick fruits for others. After the meal nobody would have to do anything. Men would share women or there would be timetable who with whom and when can have sex. Human population would grow during fertile for vegetable years and the human population would shrink during drought and climatic disaster. In case of large scale natural disasters like cosmic collision, earthquakes, super volcano eruption unprepared everybody would die.

Nobody would care for scientific discoveries. When one person would invent something nobody would care.

The whole development of our civilizasion is based on wanting to kill. Almost all scientific, technical discoveries were financed or sponsored only because someone wanted to use it in war. After a long time discoveries could be used in peaceful purpose but it is just a side effect.

This development of the technology begotten by needs for military purpose was and always is a development. Thanks that when after many years used in military would come a scare of unevitable large scale disaster the development could be used to divert the disaster or at least to ease catastrophic effects and help some people to survive such difficult times.

When one person is abusing another then the abused one has to do anything possible to defend himself, stand up against abuser or run far away to avoid abuser. The abused person is forced to increase own intellectual development and gain a new knowledge in order to survive.

What a twisted thought "The evil is not so evil after all and is helping us in longsighted look at our existence".

Quick look at religions and existence of the God.

Religions and churches as a business.

Let's say there is a righteous and honest man who mean well for everybody, never does any harm and he wants to teach, persuade others to do good only.

This man regardless of his good will has to work to provide for himself and his family. After work in free time he can spread good words. His good work and teaching are very valuable then it seams he is wasting plenty of time for regular work instead of teaching. At one point himself or after suggestion from others he decides to spend all his time to do good, on teaching good in other words he will teach about God. He still needs food, shelter for him and his family. The people listening to his teaching would start providing for him all what is necessary. Excactly in this moment pure good teaching ends and a business starts. The teacher should point out what is wrong in peoples actions but it is not nicely received because nobody neither likes to be criticized nor to change own habits when they deliver good profit. To be well provided the teacher is picking lesson in the way he would not irritate or hurt his students' feelings but at the same time he would continue to teach about goodness. Doing it this way he is receiving more and more profit, praize and fame. Those factors are causing the teacher to more and more modify the lessons to increase the profit to the max. This is the way a business works. Every church, religion is organized like a business and thanks that more and more people involved don't have to do actiual work to earn for necessities and are provided solely by growing religeus organization.

Such a religious business is getting in collision with other religious businesses and we have "holy wars" where the only purpose is to get rid of competitors and keep increasing own influence for receiving more an more lavish benefits for the leaders.

Doubts in existence of the God as misinterpretation of the definitions.

Lately Stephen Hawking said the God does not exists and property of time space fabric gives possibility to exist everything what is aroud us. As we see here credited scientists learning new scientific aspects are forgetting the basic questions.

There is no proof the God exists and there is no proof the God does not exists. We don't know if death means end of everything or there is something after the death. If there is nothing nobody will ever know. Only death people could know there is something after death if there really is something. We can only believe it is this or the other way. Every so called fact as a proof of this or that could be interpreted from higher point of view and every consideration depends only on our believe. Let's assume there is kind of life after death but it doesn't mean dead people can tell us about it or maybe for them is not worth to bother with us still living or it doesn't matter if we know what is after death.

The creation act is always introduced in metaphoric way. It is not important if the Universe, the Sun, the Earth, the people were created in few "days" or it was continous long lasting work in progress where from all species finally emerged a human being. Nobody said that our form is the latest and maybe new more advance species will emerge in the future.

Additional problem is lack of definition of God. All religions and other similar organizations have done what they could to obfuscate this subject because it gives possibilities to popularize own more beneficial interpretation.

In the first glance there are two ways to define God.

The first one is accepting God and God's act as everything what we thing as devine, unexplained, powerful beyond our imagination and all what we would like (like life after dead) it to be.

The second way is to base definition of God and information about God on ancient legends, forwarded to us messages and scripts. One of those scripts is the Bible more specifically the Torah or the Old Testament.

What today we could say about the Bible or other ancient scriptures from all places over the world seemingly not related to each other? Actually, almost nothing.

First of all those scriptures were created extremely long time ago and are written in the languages not existing and not know today. Archeologists or other researchers studying those writings are trying to decode, interpret and translate the content to current language. It is extremely difficult or impossible. The most important is problem with translation. Nobody knows well enough the ancient language of the scripts written thousands of years ago to say with 100% accuracy what everything ment. Taking in count the texts were so many times translatad from older language to newer language and from a language of one group of people to the language of another group of people. We know neither the skills of translators nor their intentions. After all those translations the texts could be completely different than originals. The original text is not so original anyway but it only is the writer's interpretation.

Just for example what in the modern English language means "hevenly body of Venus"? Does it mean the planet Venus or luscious body of the love godess?

We have to remember about the knowledge and way of thinking of the people living in time when the texts were written. Nowdays we can look at the same phenomenon differently because we have more understanding, more developed science and higher technology than our ancient ancestors.

Our level of telecommunication, audio, video transmission, airplanes flying in the air and submarines deep down under the water surface for people living a few thousands years ago would be supernatural phenomenons.

Prediction that people will have fast growing science, knowledge and will be able to travel far distances is very relative. For those who walk the horse back rider is moving very fast and very far. For transatlantic airplane travelers a space ship going to distant stars is moving fast and far. For those who don't know what a wheel is or can't ignite fire the XX century car driver has incredible knowledge. For us old automobile is nothing unusual at all.

Considering described above aspects currently living average people would seams like gods for those who lived a few thousands years ago.

Speaking about the bible and other scripts lets take another example.

In Sumerian culture people belived the Gods arrived from heaven or the sky, and they began mixing with humans what created half gods. In one interpretation someone says the Sumerian texts are telling the aliens from the Space arrived to Earth for exploitation. Later to have workers they performed genetic modification mixing monkey's and they own DNA and created humen. Later some of the aliens had children with human women. If this version is true would the aliens be the Gods since they created humen as own image?

If this is really true would we think in common understanding those aliens performing genetic modifications are gods? I don't think so. Who created the aliens? Who created the Universe?

We could in different ways interpret the second coming of the Christ. Described events could mean a space ship is coming and commander is seating with the crew members at the control center what looks like a throne. The floor is made of a transparent material. The sound like a trombon is coming from the speakers. The worthy people wearing symbolizing innocence white clothes are wearing metallic silver space suits and they are worthy because they posses useful knowledge about the Universe. The messiah stating he is the first and the last mean he as commander has the absolute power and everybody has to obey his orders. The trumpets throwing fire are some kind of guns. The four beasts could be interpreted as four robots or hybrids specialized to perform action in the air or in water or somewhere else. The scripture says only righteous will be saved. What about other righteous people? It is only matter of interpretation and this religion could mean all spiritual people. What kind of spirituality? From observation and experiences we see this spirituality means doing anything to achieve own goals. It means the smallest own profits are set higher than health, wealth or life other people. Is it really what the scripture says or is it the matter of interpretation of the translators?

Anyway we do or we don't believe in God. There is neither any proof for it nor proof against it.

How to define the term God.

Through many years and on different level of the knowledge about the Universe we can find following few definition of God:

- Having very little knowledge about the nature people were assuming that everything unknown is supernatural god's act. In this case most natural phenomenons like snow, rain, tempest, sunny wather was directly sent by a god. There were gods of the Sun, gods of the Moon, gods of the trees, gods of the animals. Including nowdays point of view all what is alive (how do we know where is the line between alive and not alive?) has inside soul as part of the God or the life in itself is a part of the God. It all sounds similar.

- The term of god could be introduced in purposedly misleading way to simplify passing the knowledge. It is possible there were ancient civilizastions on Earth but catastrophic cosmic or tectonic events wiped out the most part of the civilized race. Very few who survived were not able to live on the same level and first of all they had to survive very difficult conditions. Few or many generations later many scientific achievements were forgotten and stayed as the legends. Small number of survivors went all over the earth to more primitive groups ofpeople. The most important goal was to teach to pass the rest of the not forgotten knowledge. For those primitive tribes the civilizers had tremendous knowledge and abilities. It could happen the civilizers were assumed to be gods. What if there was following situation. The civilizers were asked "Are you Gods?" if they said "No, we are humans like you. We just hove a bit more knowledge". The primitive tribe after discussion would decide "They are like us. Let's eat them!". To avoid this kind of situation and gainig more respect and attention the civilizers could call themselve gods.

- History and archeology tell us many rulers like faroh in Egypt and many other places in the world were worshiped as gods. The rulers always have great power and in thier hands are decision for life or death of commoners. How hundreds or thousands years later supported by archeology only anybody can tell if the ruler was treated as almighty ruler or as god. Watching TV transmission from electing the Pope or from the wedding of the British Royals we cannot say if the attention is like for gods.

- Defining a god as a creator in extreme cases we could call gods all people who created something. If people were created by genetic modification then the aliens would be gods. When scientists create the first new DNA and grow something from it they would be gods too.

- According to current knowledge we don't see anything but light rays are passing the lens in our eyes and they are focuset on the sensors. The sensors change the signal to electrical one and it is all passed to the brain. All our senses are working in similar way. In result our senses create kind of virtual reality inside the brain like advanced games create virtual reality for our senses.

There is something called "I" what is receiving this virtual reality. It is possible we all are connected to very complicated computer simulator. This simulator would be controlling everything and the reality could be completely different. Maybe there is nobody else just I am and the rest is just virtual reality generated by the simulator. In such case, who created the simulator would be the God or we are just a part of the God.

- Whatever our view about the God is the human nature is not able to understand how the whole Universe is created, how it began and what is going on. There always will be the question "Who created it all?". The fabric of space is the fabric, the Universe is the Universe and in existence of the God we do believe or we don't.

Another version of cosmological theory.

After reading the latest book written by Stephen Hawking I came up with new version of idea about the Universe.

Every even the most scientific theory about the Universe is related to the idea about the God. People believe in God or not although they don't think what it means. For example we say the God is the Creator. Does it mean the person who created a car is a god too? And if using genetic modification a person can create something alive this person is a god, or at least a god for the created living thing? According to some theories the aliens performed genetic work and created human. If this is the true would those alien be gods? Not at all, we'll say after a short while of thinking.

Everybody wants to be the best, the smartest and the strongest. We the people think we are the most intelligent creatures. Many scientists agree there were humans in the past and they couldn't ignite any fire and were using very primitive tools only. Were those ancient peoples the most intelligent creatures in the world? We know and can do much more now. In few hundreds or few thousands years people will have more knowledge, skills and we will seam very primitive for them. At what point the humans are the most intelligent creatures? The human body is changing for example there is more blood types now than thousands of years ago. There could come another evolutional changes. Would our version be the most intelligent or the new one? Would current version seam not quite human for the new version?

Few thousands of years ago human knowledge was such that if todays man would show computers, TVs, phones, airplanes and everything what we think as normal than those ancients would think it is all miracle and we are gods.

There are differences between people living in the same country and very often someone says it is impossible only because the person does not know technology related to the observed subject. For example once right after the plane crash in Smolensk I told my Canadian friend the fog was man made. He answered it's impossible. Why impossible? I've seen 30 years earlier in Poland during marshal law in 1981-1982 when man made fog was often produced on much larger scale.

If we could show a scientist living few hundreds years ago one of our complicated mechanical-electrical-electronical device he would surely say it is impossible to predict what such a device could do and how it would react on external stimulus. If we could say it can be known where anybody and everybody in the world is and with what speed evey person is moving than the ancient scientist would never believe. Today although not everybody is connected to a GPS yet but we know it is possible.

In technology, chemistry, biology are many interacting factors and using current level of science it is impossible to predict with 100% accuracy what will happen with the object after described time.

Some time ago I think it was in eighties of the XX century someone from one of the American universities invented "The game in life". It was theoretical computer problem where we assume there is very large practically unlimited size field of squares similar to the chess board. At first each field could have binary value "Life" or "not alive" means empty. Next in each step of interaction we calculate the future value for each field using following rules. When empty field is touching 3 fields with "Life" the new "life" is created. When field with "Life" is touching less than 2 other fields with "Life" then it dies of loneliness and become empty. From a computer simulation of this game we've learned that depends on beginning status of the fields the "life" is flickering forth and back or it is growing and sometimes it creates very interesting patterns moving a cross the field. The more contacting fields with "Life" we have the more complicated configurations are creating and changing. It was only theoretical game where results could be predicted by a computer to some level. Let's remember how many living cells are in our body and how many atoms are included in one cell...

When someone could kind of create a kind of universe as an image projected from a film to the screen than the living creature on such screan could do any scientific research about their Universe. They would see they can move in they world and there are other object which can change positions. After carefull observation they would see when one object is coming so close to the other that they began taking the same space than one of the objects (we would call it background) disappeares and in this particular place is only the second object (we would call it foreground). In farther research of the geometry the screen creature would see although they perceive their Universe in two dimensions they actually live in three dimension (because the screen is not very flat) because the distances between points are different than it would be in two dimensional world. Later they would discover grains of the screan what for them would be similar to our world on atomic size level. The grains of the screan and the angle of the light form the projector would cause tiny shadows. They would see the light is not only on the surface but sometimes it bounces from uneven part of the screen to the other near by spots. If they would do more research on geometry, lighted surface the way we are discovering our Universe is built as a wave and as a mass who knows maybe they could figure out there is the screen and distant light source projecting an image on the almost flat screen.

In more and more accurate observation there is more and more interaction between the observer and the object because the observer, the object and method of observation is in the same world using the same fabric. At one point more accurately we want to measure something the more our interaction is changing the world and the Heisenberg's uncertainty principle is coming to our attention.

We do remember from the previous considerations the game in "Life" where computers almost could predict next steps in the game life. We could think there is much higher intelligence. They can build such a powerful computer to predict step by step all states in our Universe. Just by knowing the nature laws like electromagnetism, gravitation, weak and strong interaction plus some more unknown to us and knowing the starting point in observation. They could predict every position of every atom or subatomic particle, energy, waves from the big bang to todays positions and farther. Our Universe could be just a small experiment for those beings. To observe our projector and screen experiment we watch the light bounced from the screen.

In case of observing our universe the presence of the observer would intreract a lot in observed universe.

The scientists are telling us we don't really see anything but light rays as electromagnetic waves are passing through our eyes. The lens in the eye is focusing image of the objects on the light sensors. The sensors are changing it to electrical signals send to our brain. Inside the brain are electrical images of the light coming from the real objects. In similar way acustic waves are converted and create images inside our brain. We could say all our senses are just creating kind of virtual reality inside our brain. There is the I who is sensing, perceiving this virtual reality. We can think there is no real world but there is just the virtual reality what we feel and live in. We could seriously consider that our senses are connected to reality simulator. This simulator is giving us all we see, hear, feel and provides our interaction. If the simulator is sophisticated enough it would be very difficult or impossible to recognize it and we could live in a "Matrix" without ever knowing it. Going farther it is possible that all of you, all animals, plants, planets, stars don't exist at all and there is only one "I" living in the virtual reality provided by the simulator.

Let's come to the conclusion what is this version of the Universe by adding all pieces together.

In this theory which is as unchecked and unproved as all other so called scientific theories the whole universe is just an experiment, simulation of much more complicated version of "the game in life". Our every person's "I" is just the way to observe the simulated universe. This "I" is observing with very little interaction because the "I" is kind of spiritual perceiving all particles, waves and energy movements as virtual reality. Maybe this whole simulation experiments has created live plants, animals and people just to observe the experiment.

I placed this theory here only to show that this crazy story is as serious and scientific as all other commonly accepted theories about the Universe. This story like all those scientific theories is completely unchecked and unproved. This story is actually better than many others because I made it up in 5 minutes after reading the latest book written by Stephen Hawking and I based my theories on other sucked from the thumb theories.

Why people do harm to the others.

Everybody wants to be special, exceptional, respected, important and popular. Actually everybody wants to have sex with the most attractive partners, eat the most tasteful and nutritious food and have easy and pleasant life.

To have an easy life one has to become a leader of a group of people. The larger the group is the more benefits the leader can receive.

Can you become a leader by doing good for people? Of course not. When one does only good things for someone than the other person likes it for a short while. Later it is all forgotten and the person feels uneasy and aversion to the benefactor because we don't like to be dependent of others.

The Jesus Christ did not become any leader and was killed.

Let's take an example when someone would do something very good without asking for anything in return. Let's say the person can cure any including the worse disease. The sick people would keep coming for help and later they would forget about the healer. Of course the healer would not die of hunger because from time to time someone would give him a food just in case the healer could be needed to cure another future sickness. This good acting person would live on a verge of poverty. When a very rich person with terminal disease would get cured I'm sure after the fact he would not give his wealth to the healer.

On the other hand every good acting shortly becomes normality in the eyes of others and the charity work is expected to be continued. When this person needs some help from others he is forgotten.

Nobody can become very rich just by doing good for hire either. The payment will be smaller and smaller and employer will do anything possible to demean value of the employee's work.

The easier way to have an easy and great life is to take everything from others. The most people are promoted because they do not do too good work on the current position and it is not important for superiors to keep the person in the same place. It could be beneficial to send poor employee higher and get someone better in their place. The employee doing very well the job will never be promoted because the boss is not stupid. Why to promote someone good and lose this good employee. Nobody knows how good the replacement worker would be then it is not worth the risk.

No person can by himself work out enough goods to have great life.

Only becoming a leader of the large group gives the chance. The leader keeps the group in iron hand usually by obvious or conditional scare. The leader very often uses part of the group to do harm to all others and to take everybody's wealth and give it to the leader. The leaders always take all kind of benefits away from everybody but to encourage someone or to force someone to do more effort the leaders take a bit less.

When we want any personal achievement like performing required task well and quick, breaking a previous record in sport it would seam the result depends on us only. Unfortunately it isn't so. There is always someone who at all cost with the whole power will try to prevent our goal. For example when we perform our job task correctly and fast someone else doing it longer would look bad in the superior's eye. In case of sport records there are people who benefit from their favorite's winnings and they do anything to eliminate us.

Getting to do any task or achieving any goal we have to remember there are always unexpected problems and difficulties because nobody knows anything perfectly and there are other who with all the power will be getting in our way. We have to conquer the challenge of the task and to defeat artificial problems created by competition. We should never give up and step by step go to the target. As they say "It's not over until is over".

A medicine to cure humanity not to cure from humanity.

The most people in their lives were thinking at least once what should be done to make the lives of all people better, safer, richer. What one could do having unlimited magical powers.

In such cases we usually end up thinking that we should remove (this way or the other) all the worse people who do harm to others. To remove the people who are causing wars, unjustice and abuse on large scale.

Unfortunately removing the worse ones would not help much. It could help for very short while only but later the other mean spirited would take the place and they would do the same harm to others.

The only cure for people is to make them understand that everybody should always stick to the following rule:

Don't do to others what you don't want others do to you. Don't do it even if you derive a lot of pleasure from it.

Moon Landing.

Have they go to the Moon or they haven't.

Americans and Russians were competitors in conquering the Space. It seams both countries were on the similar technical level. All spies were working hard then most often one discovery on one side was shortly known to the competitors. They wanted to lead in achievements. Finally the Russian sent out Sputnik to the orbit.

Another day Americans widely promoted future landing the men on the Moon. On TV in most countries there was live transmission showing how a man walked and long jumped on the surface of the Moon. The main proof was installation of a mirror on the Moon. The mirror was reflecting back light rays sent from the Earth what let calculate the distance to the Moon more accurately.

The less interesting fact was the cosmonauts took a few pictures on the Moon and brough them back to the Earth. The pictures were published and very often commented. The problem is the camera taking picture on the Moon would be exposed out there and on the way up as well as on the way down to the cosmic radiation. The cosmic radiation would overexpose the film to make it useless. We have been warned for years that security systems at the airport gates can damage the film. Sure it is possible to bild a camera where the film would not be exposed to the cosmic rays what would make the film save. Yes, it would be possible only if anybody knows about cosmic radiation at that time.

The mirror on the Moon could be installed by unmanned space craft which came close enough and dropped the mirror down to the surface.

Another fact against manned moon landing is the Americans were keep going to the Moon for a few years. As soon as Russian constructed radar equipment allowing them to trace the space ships the Americans ceased men flying to the Moon and didn't do it ever again in the next 30 years. On the other hand the Russian never went to the Moon at all.

The whole Moon landing story is so similar to the book written by Jules Verne with similarity of the events and the names. I think someone directing the "moon landing" hoax based it on the Jules Verne book "From the Earth to the Moon".

Why nobody informed the public about it.

The Russian didn't go to the Moon and they didn't cry about it. They most likely knew that American Moon landing was just a hoax and they didn't need to compete with fairy tale. They didn't say about it because it was better to know the truth and keep it quiet. Did the Americans new that the Russian knew? Most likely, yes. In a poker game is good to know that other players don't have a good card and is bluffing only. On the other hand not spreading the news was a courtesy related to the Sputnik orbiting the Earth. This Sputnik was a ball about 2m (6ft) in diameter with few devices inside. The whole world was admiring it, the astronomers were watching it but nobody mentioned the real Sputnik is so small it cannot be seen using less professional equipment. Many amateur astronomers were watching something shiny orbiting the Earth. Neither Russian nor Americans ever said the people are watching just the thrown away parts of the engines used to send out the Sputnik on the orbit.

Time travel.

Small philosophy.

Einstein invented relativity theory and described many principles using light and based on the speed of the light. This model is very good in many cases but...

We could have a theory that our brains/souls/personalities all what we feel is not for real but it is just connected to a great simulator like it was shown in the movie "Matrix". Ths computer simulator stimulates everything what we feel. This simulator is so sophisticated it can synchronize feelings of all of us.

Going farther I can think there are no any you at all. It is just one I connected to the simulator. All stimuluses persuade me about all reality and I am drowing conclusions from it. I meet other theories invented by other people but actually it is all coming from the simulator only to make my experiences more interesting for me. There are the theories I don't understand and the theories I've never heard of or they don't exist and the simulator is just telling me there is something I don't know to push me into advancing.

Traveling in time.

As far as I understand many of the modern scientific theories are based on the electromagnetic waves and on the speed of light. When something is moving faster and faster with a speed close to the speed of light than the mass of it is getting bigger and bigger. To change movement of a mass we have to use a force and the change in movements depends on the power of the force and the mass of the object. Since the faster the object moves the bigger its mass is we need to use larger and larger force to speed it up more. Reaching the speed of light the mass of the object is infinitly big and we would need infinitly large force to speed it up a bit more. The conclusion is nothing can travel faster than light.

In the other part of the theory the present is define as where at this moment the light would reach what is good in many calculations but it messes with our heads.

The light is spreading in straight lines and the mass is curving the space time.

We could imagine a space time where going from one point to the other we can use two different length ways. Sending the light the longer way the light ray will reach the second point after some time. When considered space time is so much curved that we could use the second shorter way and reach the destination in shorter time than the light do it the first way. It could happen we would arrive to the destination before would the light going the longer way. It would mean we traveled back in time since we see ourseve sending the signal after we are already at the destination.

Really?

What about the other light ray travelling the same way we do? How can we tell wich light ray defines the present and which the future?

This is like with the old computer definitions for the year. The year was marked with the last two digits only. In this way year 1995 was represented by "95" only and year 2015 was represented by "15". In this computer model the date 2015 is lower or older than 1995. All algotithms would work correctly but what it has to do with reality? Whatever the reality means?

We, looking far away at the light years distant stars see them the way we do. This is our present. Because it took the light thousands of years to travel from the stars to us the position of those stars is completely different and we see where the stars were thousands of years ago. Some say that from our relative point of view the stars are where the light coming from them points us to. From the star point of view the star is somewhere else because it was keep moving for thousands of years.

This is working only in theory when we defined the present in the wrong way. Who cares about the ray of the light?

Traveling in fake way in time means we sent from originating point light the longer way to the destination and we traveled the sorter way. We arrive at the destination before the light we sent but it doesn't mean we traveled in time. It means our definition of the present based on the light is incorrect.

We can consider as well that events from the traveling light point of view have different sequence.

We could twist this theory and say that our experiment created another paralel reality because from the light ray point of view happened what could not happen.

On the other hand when we assume the reality is what our senses perceive than defining something what we think as time and basing it on the speed of light does not fit our reality.

Let's reconsider famous traveling twins. The one was moving across more gravitational forces and after return he is younger than the other twin. One of the twins' watches went farther than the other watch.

Let's this time put one twin into the fridge and to hibernate him. After many years we can thaw him and he would be in the same aged as he was before freezing. Could we say one of the twins traveled in time? No! One of the twins was exposed to conditions where he was getting older much slower than the other twin.

The same is with twins traveling with a speed close to speed of light. It doesn't mean the one twin traveled in time but it means the one was exposed to conditions where he was getting older slower than the other twin.

Looking at the traveling twins we measure time as number of heart beats or tics in the watch. Every twin moving with different speed could have different number of tics but when they meet again they are in the same reality at the same time the difference is in amount of experiences they've had.

Maybe we just have incorrect definition of time based on the speed of light?

The paralel universes? Of course they are. Having time definition based on the speed of light everybody lives in own parallel universe because we are in different spots in space and it takes different length of time for the light to reach each of us. We perceive the same events in different sequence. For example light from the star A comes to one person first and to the second person later on the other hand light from the star B comes to second person first and to the first person later. Those two people experience the same events in different sequence means they must live in different could be parallel universes.

If this is parallel universes let's be happy we've just discovered it.

We can travel in time on a daily basis. I did it by myself. Once on a Pacific cruise there was the January 14th in the open ocean. Later we crossed the date line and arrived to Fanning Island which is in the Republic Kiribati where was already the January 15th. After half day of fun we left, crossed the date line again and we had the January 14th again. I was moving forward in time and then I was moving backward in time.

I wish you all nice time in time travel!

Conclusion

When a person has two choices:

- The first choice

    This person situation will get better but another man situation will get much better

- The second choice

    This person situation will get worse but another person situation will get much worse

he usually picks the second choice. He hurts a lot but is happy that someone else is hurting more.

Stanislaw Lem once described in his book **the unit of pleasure**.

The unit of pleasure for a person is when having a rock in own shoe one is walking a distance of 1 km and then takes the rock out of own shoe, places it in the friend's shoe and then is observing while the friend with the rock in the shoe is walking a distance 1 km.

This type of behavior and thinking cannot be natural.

We can say with great probability that some pseudo scientists are right saying the aliens arrived on Earth and began genetic modifications on humans. The experiment went sour and we are what we are.

That's all falks.

I wish you all plenty of pleasure!

Boleslaw Tabor wrote this book using own life experiences plus some research and study.

It all started as a bunch of emails sent to friends. Most of the information is related to America were in English. All combined together became a book with titles and chapters.

In the next step everything was translated to Polish.

There were plans to translate it to the French language too but there was not enough time to do it.

Some graphic designs should be used to make the book more attractive. On the other hand the most important and valuable is the most boring part of the book. The author has chosen very limited graphics. The simple black and white form emphasizes that content of this book is not very fancy. The title promises something very controversial what at first would seem twisted but after short consideration the readers could accept it as some kind of truth.